The Revelation

of

God in History

by
John F. Haught

WIPF & STOCK · Eugene, Oregon

To Evelyn,
and my sons, Paul and Martin

Wipf and Stock Publishers
199 W 8th Ave, Suite 3
Eugene, OR 97401

The Revelation of God in History
By Haught, John F.
Copyright©1988 by Haught, John F.
ISBN 13: 978-1-60608-420-5
Publication date 12/17/2008
Previously published by Michael Glazier, 1988

TABLE OF CONTENTS

1

The Idea of Revelation

"It's all so one-sided."

A well known theologian recalls a time when, after delivering a sermon on trust and doing God's will, he was challenged by a member of the congregation. "You speak," the latter said, "of trusting God, of praying to Him and doing His will. But *it's all so one-sided.* We speak to God, we bow down before Him and lift up our hearts to Him. But He never speaks to us. He makes no sign. *It's all so one-sided.*"[1] Probably many other believers have had the same complaint.

In the Scriptures, however, we read over and over again the words: "Listen!", "If you but listen to the voice of the Lord...," if you remain alert and attentive you will hear something after all. The imperative to "hearken," to remain receptive to a revelatory "word" is pervasive in the Hebrew and Christian (as well as the Islamic) texts. Although the notion of revelation does not appear formally within the Bible (and in fact does not become a central theme of theology until after the Enlightenment), the sacred writings and traditions all invite us to listen closely, and they promise that we shall hear a word bearing good news. The idea of revelation, then, is by implication a dominant, overarching theme in biblically based religious traditions. And yet, those of us who profess allegiance

[1]John Baillie, *The Idea of Revelation in Recent Thought* (New York: Columbia University Press, 1956), p. 137.

5

to these traditions cannot always suppress a sense that no matter how hard we listen, we often do not hear anything:

> Ah yes, we may reply, that would indeed be an experience to enjoy, but is it really available to us? It is well enough to invite us to listen, but what if, when we do listen, we hear nothing? That, we may say, is the root of our trouble. Hearken we ever so diligently, we are rewarded only with a stony silence. After all, has not mankind listened attentively enough through these thousands of years? How men have searched for God! How that old firmament above us has been scanned on starry nights with all the agony of prayer! How the paths of logic have been scoured and scoured again, if haply they might reveal some sign or hint of the divine reality! And what, we may ask, has been the result but a tense and oppressive silence? That Sphinx in the Egyptian desert is the true representation of Deity. Upon our stormy questionings it turns its inscrutable, expressionless face; but no one has ever heard it speak.[2]

. Those who are familiar with Western religious traditions have been instructed repeatedly that the content of these faiths has been "revealed" to us. Christian, Jewish and Islamic faiths are said to be rooted in a "revelation" that we would hear clearly if we would but hearken. The Scriptures are said to be the "revealed" word of God. And history is said to be the explicit locus of God's revelation. But what is this "revelation?" What does "God's revelation in history" really mean? How could we hear it if it is indeed addressed to us? What difference would it make to us? In the final analysis, aren't things a bit one-sided after all?

Christians traditionally have believed that God has spoken clearly enough, first in the creation of the world, second in the history of Israel, and finally in Jesus the Christ. According to this tradition, if there is any one-sidedness it is on God's part.

[2] *Ibid.*, pp. 136-37.

There is an overwhelming fullness to God's word to us, but a troubling feebleness in our attentiveness. In traditional Christian faith there is no hesitation in affirming constantly that a "word" has been sent to us, that things are not one-sided, that our questions and pleas are not projected into a vacuum. But can we really believe this, and especially can we believe it today?

The most general claim that believers make for "revelation" is that "somehow" it makes things make sense for us. It ties together the world of our experience in a manner that would be impossible without revelation. Without the "stories of God" that form the content of biblical religion much of reality would be unintelligible. Revelation (from the Latin *revelare*, "to remove the veil") narratively illuminates reality so that we can see it more clearly than by reason or ordinary experience alone. It gives us a sense of who we are, both socially and individually. And it gives us hope. This, at any rate, is how "revelation" appears to its alleged recipients. But what is it? Precisely how does it "work?" Is it trustworthy and truthful? Why isn't it obvious to everyone? Is the notion of revelation even credible today—especially the doctrine of a divine revelation in history? Why would revelation be given to a particular people at a particular time? How can we be expected to believe that a God of all would be so partial in imparting revelation only to a few? In short, doesn't it seem that the idea of revelation has become untenable today, at least for many people in the modern world?

If this book is to be of any interest to the reader, who has perhaps been bothered by some of these same questions, it must take them into account. And, rather than being a simple repetition of remote and abstract doctrines, it must be addressed to real concerns rather than artificial problems devised by remote theological abstraction. If the idea of revelation is to be at all plausible or significant to us, it must be understood in terms of those questions that are most important to us. And if our discussion is to have any value it must deal with issues that preoccupy us at this particular time in the universe's and society's history. If we fail to relate our topic to such issues we are not doing theology in an appropriate way. For, in a sense, the question of the possibility of doing theology today coincides with the question of the very plausibility of revelation.[3]

I shall attempt here to think about the notion of revelation in a fresh manner. Of course I will have to draw upon the many rich studies of revelation that have been written both in the past and in recent years by significant theologians. But I do not intend simply to repeat their ideas nor to make this book a mere summary and classification of the various theories on our subject. In any case, such studies have already been competently written by others. Instead I shall commence almost as though we have never even heard of the notion of revelation at all. The first part of each chapter will sketch an aspect of our situation in the world as if this situation had never been illuminated by a revelatory word. And the second part of each chapter will discuss the meaning of revelation in terms of the analysis given in the first part. Obviously our cultural situation has already been shaped by images and ideas flowing from what Christians would call revelation, and our concrete questions arise out of a context that has been deeply influenced by biblical motifs. But our questions are nevertheless signals of our fundamental uncertainty and our longing for a clearer vision of the reality in which we dwell. It is important therefore that we first bring our questions and uncertainties out into the open. Using this method of beginning with our own immediate questions we might be able to grasp the significance of "God's revelation in history" in a more dramatic fashion than if we started by merely giving definitions and then elaborating on them. And in this way we shall be able to "correlate" any possible revelatory pattern of meaning with the actual questions that preoccupy many of us today.[4]

What then are our uncertainties? In what way do we still live in darkness? We can ask these questions meaningfully only if we first become aware of our "situation," that is, the context out of which our questions arise. It is obviously impossible for

[3] Heinrich Fries, *Revelation* (New York: Herder & Herder, 1969), p. 19.

[4] This method of "correlation" has been proposed most explicitly by Paul Tillich. It has recently been endorsed and revised by David Tracy who insists that any correlation of revelation with our human questions be "critically" undertaken.

us to cover every aspect of our situation, but we can at least delineate six major areas.

1. *The cosmic context.* We exist first of all as inhabitants of a vast and expanding universe that originated fifteen to twenty billion years ago in a mysterious event which scientists today call the "Big Bang." We shall call this first arena of questioning the *cosmic context* of our existence. Most of science today maintains that our universe is in "evolution," that through billions of years it has gradually unfolded, starting from pre-atomic elements and then moving through atomic, molecular, living and now conscious developments. It is difficult for those of us who have become even superficially familiar with recent cosmology to suppress certain fundamental questions: why is the world an evolutionary movement rather than a stationary, immobile mass? What is the meaning of this evolution? Is there any purpose to the universe? Does it have any aim or discernible directionality? Where do we go to find any intelligibility in this bewildering world-in-process? These are some of the questions we shall address in Chapter 1. There we shall ask whether the notion of a divine revelation in history helps us in our understanding of what sort of reality the universe is.

2. The *historical context.* We also belong to the *history* of the human species. *Homo sapiens* has been living in our terrestrial sector of the cosmos for less than a million years. Through most of this time humans have dwelt in isolated tribal arrangements in proximity to nature. It was not until some-where between eight to five thousand years ago that this tribal existence gradually gave way in certain regions to broader and more complex social arrangements that eventually led to the great civilizations, nations and cultures of more recent times. At some time in the relatively recent past, perhaps several thousand years ago, some peoples began to develop a consciousness not only of living in nature but also in history. And as this historical consciousness began to emerge, the question of meaning in history arose along with it. In our own times this question of the meaning of history has reached a climax of urgency. Hundreds of ideologies, the most obvious being Marxism, have attempted to answer this question. Visionaries galore have tried to instruct us on where history is

headed. The plurality of positions on this issue has caused a confusion that leads some to despair, and others back to nature. Does history have any meaning to it? Where does the sense of living in history come from in the first place? How are we to understand our historical identity? Is history leading us in any discernible direction? These are just some of the questions we shall deal with in Chapter 3.

3. *The social context.* Human history has been a chronicle of upheavals followed by some stability followed by yet more turmoil. Our sometimes tranquil circumstances can easily cause us to repress the memory of the millions of people both today and in the past who have been displaced, slaughtered and eventually forgotten throughout human history's painful transitions. The events we read about in history books tell about the lives of only a very few of our fellow human beings. And most of the time the histories have been written by the conquerors. But what about the rest? What about the lives and sufferings of those countless forgotten victims of history's brutality? Is there any significance to their suffering? Is there any redemption from it? Where can we turn for answers to these questions? Are there any answers available?

And what about the situation of poverty and hunger in the world today? Most of us live our lives as members of a nationalistically organized society. Or we probably belong at least to one nation more focally than to others. One of the most determinative characteristics of the nations of the world is their economic status. We know today, much more vividly than did our philosophical and theological predecessors, how important economic arrangements are in shaping the values, ideologies and cultures of various states. Our ways of thinking and relating to others, our most important ideals, are not arrived at independently of economic factors. Members of North American society in particular are faced with some very difficult questions today. These questions arise most obviously out of our situation of belonging to a social framework that has already opted for an economic system whose policies often have questionable implications for the poor within our own country and in other nations. How do our economic arrangements affect the concrete lives of the poor and the people of other nations, and how do they influence the international economic situation? These questions, it will be observed, all converge on the issue of justice. But what is justice—in its deepest dimensions? What would constitute the most just arrangements of our social, political and economic structures? How would a more just economic framework affect our consciousness, and how would a consciousness shaped by justice influence these structures? Does "revelation" have anything significant to say to what is perhaps the most pressing concern in our world today, the demand for justice? And what are we to make of the forgotten sufferings of injustice by the millions who have preceded us and who are usually left out of our attempts to understand history? Does the notion of revelation help us in our quest for some answer to the problem of suffering and injustice in society? This question of suffering and social justice, though far beyond anything that we can discuss adequately in this short book, will be the subject matter of Chapter 4. There we shall also make mention of the terror of possible nuclear annihilation and seek to position this seemingly desperate situation in terms of the idea of revelation.

4. *The religious context.* Throughout the ages most people have been participants in what we now call "religion." The religious "situation" is inseparable from human existence as such. Religion as an expression of and response to the sense of "mystery" or a "sacred" reality seems to be nearly universal. Most people up until modern times—and here the exceptions are often intellectuals in university communities—have had an explicit sense of some "other dimension," a sense of the sacred, the divine, the numinous, or what we shall call, in a general way, mystery. And even in secular cultures today there is the search for something "ultimate" (even if it be something purely material or secular) to trust in or to worship. The sense of "God" may have been lost or may have at least diminished in some corners of modern consciousness, but the religious tendency to seek some manifestation of ultimacy has not perished. And religion as a sense of mystery still abides, even though the awareness of mystery is often repressed to some degree. Religiousness in this broad sense of an encounter with "mystery" seems to be a most durable aspect of our human situation. And out of this dimension of our existence arises a fascinating set of questions: what is the deepest meaning of the

mystery that surrounds our birth and death in this universe? What is the mystery really like at heart? Is it fundamentally unknowable, fathomless, inexpressible, unintelligible, sphinx-like? Or does it have a face that we can relate to in a personal way? Is the mystery in which we are embedded indifferent to us, or does it draw near to us in caring intimacy? Where do we turn for an answer to this perennial question? Is there an answer? Or is the ageless religious sense of the mysterious destined for shipwreck on the rocks of a totally secularistic interpretation of the world? What is the relation, if any, between the human sense of mystery and the Christian's belief in a special historical revelation? As I shall argue in Chapter 5, we all have some sense of mystery (even if we call it by other names), but we long to know more about it. What does "revelation" mean in relation to our pervasive human sense of mystery?

5. *The personal context.* There is also what may be called the personal dimension of our existence. As individuals we have many concerns that we share with others who exist alongside us in the above-mentioned contexts. But there is an aspect of our being that we cannot completely share with others. It is our deeply private, personal and incommunicable "selfhood." Out of this hidden selfhood come perhaps the most urgent of our concerns. I am referring especially to what has been called the "quest for meaning," the "quest for freedom" or the "search for identity." Whatever we choose to call it, it is an attempt to find an answer to the eternal questions: who am I in the deepest core of my selfhood? Do I fit in anywhere in a complete way? Do I fully belong to any context that I can clearly identify? How do I satisfy my longing for significance? Though my personal quest may be satisfied partly by my participating in the other five of our six contexts, there is still a residue of individuality that cannot be grasped in terms of an analysis of any of them. Would an historical revelation assist me in any way in this very personal quest? In Chapter 6 we shall look at this question in more detail.

6. *The critical context.* Many of us also belong to communities searching after "truth." I am myself part of a university which, like all academic institutions, considers itself to be a community attempting to arrive at a reasonable understanding

of things. This society of scholars and teachers is concerned that we not only have an understanding, but above all a *critical* understanding of things. This means that we must always be ready to revise our understanding as new data come into the sweep of our experience. We must follow a fruitful method, such as science, if we are to arrive at the truth. The desire to know the truth is for many the most intense and irrepressible of all human longings. Some are willing to sacrifice a great deal for the sake of what they take to be the "truth." But what is truth? Are we sure that we already know what it is? How would we recognize it when we come upon it? Above all, how can we keep our desire for truth from being consumed by other desires that are not at all interested in the truth? In what sort of context is our desire for the truth most capable of surviving and even thriving? Is the quest for truth compatible with our having any sort of faith in revelation? Or would not such faith interfere with or distract us from any disinterested searching for objectivity and truth? We shall deal with this question, often referred to as the question of *reason and revelation*, in Chapter 7.

The perspective I bring to the topic of revelation is shaped by my own sense of belonging to these six circles: cosmos, history, society, mystery, personality and critical inquiry. Of course these circles all overlap and interpenetrate, but out of each of the six there arise distinct questions. And the structure of this book will follow the patterns of questioning that come from each diverse context. In each of the following six chapters I shall attempt, in a very sketchy way, to present the significance of the Christian notion of an historical revelation in terms of the issues that emerge from our reflecting on the six circles that constitute our situation.

Recent Theologies of Revelation

In the history of theology "revelation" has often been understood as an inner "illumination" or as a sort of divine teaching and instruction. At other times it has been understood according to a "propositional" model. That is, "revelation" has been taken to be the communication of information capable of being expressed in sentences or propositions. Today, however, the central model for understanding the idea of revelation has shifted to a more "personal" one, at least in most important theological reflection. Revelation is understood by theology today, and especially Catholic theology, fundamentally as God's *self*-revelation. It is first of all the gift of God's own self, and only derivatively is it the propositional unfolding of the event of this divine self-gift. Revelation is not primarily the uncovering of information that is otherwise inaccessible to reason and ordinary experience. Such a "gnostic" idea, tempting though it has been since very early in the history of Christianity, trivializes the idea of revelation, making it appeal more to our sense of curiosity than to our need for transformation and hope. Instead revelation means essentially God's gift of self. And the awareness of such a self-giving God is "revealed" to faith not as a proposition or doctrine but as a *promise* of ultimate fulfillment. The sense of God's revelation in history happened first to people whose lives swelled with a sense of expectation. Today as well, any meaningful sense of revelation would occur only to those of us who can share this same sense of promise and the hope that accompanies it.

Revelation is not as complicated or as magical as we might once have suspected. In its depth it is an exceedingly simple notion, though that does not make it any easier to accept and understand. As Karl Rahner has often emphasized, revelation means fundamentally the communication of the mystery of God to the world. This divine self-communication influences the world at every phase of its coming-to-be, and not just at the human level of propositional understanding nor within the confines of the biblical world alone. Revelation is a constant, ongoing outpouring of God's creative, formative love into the world. In this sense it has a "general" character, and in some way every being is affected (and even constituted) by this universal divine self-communication. Thus the idea of revelation in contemporary theology tends to converge with the biblical theme of creation. Creation itself is already the self-revelation of God.

However, biblical faith has influenced theologians to speak also of "revelation in history," "historical revelation," or "special revelation" in addition to God's universal or "general" self-revelation. In the history of Israel and in the person of Jesus of Nazareth, Christians believe that God who is present to the world everywhere and at all times manifests the divine essence in a unique and definitive way.

While Christians celebrate the apparently "exceptional" divine self-disclosure in Christ, the notion of a "special" revelation in history is today the source of much controversy. To those who approach the world out of what I have called the "critical context," which has been deeply influenced by the scientific revolution and the Enlightenment's emphasis on "reason," the idea of a unique revelation by a universal God to a specific people in a limited historical setting seems magical and mythical. It raises the question as to whether one can be a devotee of biblical revelation while at the same time accepting the norms of reason and critical consciousness. Can the truly enlightened person concerned with a critical, objective grasp of truth honestly accept a unique historical revelation? I shall attempt to express the consensus of much recent theology (Jewish, Protestant and Catholic) that the idea of revelation in history does not imply a magical intrusion of foreign information, as is often imagined in popular piety. In its deepest, promissory essence revelation is the opening of the universe to the very possibility of a truly historical mode of existence. Such an interpretation of revelation need not conflict with the legitimate demands of reason.

The idea of a special historical revelation is also problematic to many who dwell within the broad "religious context" of human experience. Although they are quite willing to agree that all people are always touched by the *mystery* that surrounds our existence, they see no need to posit a special and decisive historical revelation of this mystery. And they are sometimes suspicious of the apparent pretentiousness of those who do.[5] There is a refining edge to this objection, and theology today must take it into account. A certain triumphalism and sense of superiority has been a strong temptation to biblical religions grounded in the doctrine of

---

[5]The German philosopher, Karl Jaspers, is one of the best-known advocates of this position. See, for example, Karl Jaspers and Rudolf Bultmann, *Myth and Christianity*, trans. by N. Guterman (New York: Noonday Press, Inc., 1958).

special revelation. Although there are strong warnings against such inflation in the scriptures and traditions of these religions, a theology of revelation today has to be especially sensitive to the accusations of special privilege.

In order to offset the impression of any such arrogance in the present work I would once again point the reader to what is considered by many Christian theologians today to be the primary meaning of revelation: God's gift of self to the *world*. Such a formula prohibits our restricting this gift to a specific people or to a specific church community. Revelation in its fundamental meaning is universal. If we still continue to speak of a *historical* revelation we do not mean that it is special in the sense that the people to whom it is communicated are thereby superior to other human beings. Nor does it mean that they are any more significant in the sight of God. Even though it inevitably bears the marks of particularity, a feature that is inseparable from the Christian doctrine of the incarnation, the idea of God's revelation in history means something much deeper, more universal and less pretentious than these suspicions suggest. Hence the theme of revelation as God's self-gift with *universal* intent will be a constant one in each of this book's chapters.

Because the notion of revelation seems to suggest a particularity that overrides the contemporary trend toward ecumenism and universalism, some recent theology has become altogether embarrassed about the idea. It has at times even suggested that revelation is a notion that any respectable theology of the future will have to learn to live without if it is to avoid triumphalism and religious imperialism. It is difficult to imagine how belief in historical revelation can be abandoned without destroying the very foundations of biblical religion, but every effort must be made to remove from the idea any shadow of arrogance. Therefore, I would suggest that the most important reason for our clinging to the notion of revelation is not to evoke a sense of privilege but to give strong expression to our sense of the always surprising intitiative or "prevenience" of God and the conviction that we are not ourselves the authors of the promise we live by. The notion of revelation is indispensable for giving expression to the experience of our being encountered again and again by a mystery of promise that is by its very nature radically surprising, new and unpredictable when viewed according to our ordinary standards of expectation. If we lose the notion of revelation we lose a sense that we are being addressed and invited by something beyond ourselves. And when we lose that impression of being challenged by the mystery of the transcendent, our world becomes closed in on itself in a way that is too suffocating for the human spirit. The idea of revelation, among its other attributes, preserves the intuition that an unanticipated dimension of utter surprisingness lies before us and beyond our capacity to control.

Revelation has nothing to do with the superiority of one religious group over another. Rather it is about the surprise that awaits us all and which none of our most creative imaginings and projections can come close to representing adequately. Revelation is a goad to our consciousness, urging it to strive constantly to imagine anew the ultimate context of our existence. But it is at the same time a judgment upon the inadequacy of any of these imaginings, and it is also a powerful stimulus to reach out further and further to the mystery that invites us into its incomprehensible grasp. If we keep before us the self-revising imperative given by revelation we can hardly fall into the complacency of which opponents of the idea are understandably apprehensive.

A Word about Method

Theology has to follow a method. And if it is interested in arriving at appropriate results it should be self-conscious about its method. Especially since the birth of modern science the various disciplines have become more and more sensitive to the need to be methodical in order to arrive at appropriate results. And contemporary theology is one such discipline.

The word "method" comes from the Greek *méta hódos*, meaning "according to a way or path." The term implies that if truth is to be found then certain rules must be followed. The road to truth cannot be trodden indiscriminately. We must somehow plan our assault on the subject matter of our various disciplines. Bernard Lonergan has defined method as a "set of directives guiding a process to a result," and today theology struggles to find the appropriate directives for dealing with its own peculiar subject matter, revelation.

In the present century there have emerged two opposing positions regarding theological method and how to approach the subject of revelation in particular. One of these has been proposed by the Swiss theologian, Karl Barth. Barth argues that we should not approach revelation with any predetermined method. For if we do we shall surely shrink and distort the subject matter of faith in order to make it fit our own presuppositions. Instead we should let revelation encounter us and take hold of us without our planning any sort of methodical approach to it. Let revelation bring its own method along with it instead of imposing one of our own making upon it.

The importance of Barth's position lies in the fact that it insists on the initiative of God as the author of revelation. It maintains that revelation is always infinitely more than anything we could conjure up in our own minds. The promise given in revelation must be seen as independent of all our human wishing. It must retain its surprising, gratuitous and shocking substance if it is to function as revelation. This emphasis on the primacy of God is perhaps Barth's most significant contribution to modern theology. And it is important that we always remain in touch with this aspect of his thought.

However, in order to preserve the sense of God's initiative in revelation, there is no good reason to suppress our concern with being methodical. Rudolf Bultmann, who represents the opposing position, insists on the necessity of method in theology. He says that method is nothing other than a way of putting questions.[6] In order for the content of revelation to make any sense to us it must respond to real questions and proccupations that we already have. If revelation does not respond to our own questions, then how could we possibly "hearken" to it? It is our questions that make us look for some

[6]Rudolf Bultmann, *Jesus Christ and Mythology* (New York: Charles Scribner's Sons, 1958) p. 49-50.

revelatory answer in the first place.

Thus theology must also attend to the business of shaping our questions appropriately if we are to be exposed to the relevant aspects of revelation. The shape of the questions guiding our inquiry determines, in some vague way at least, the kind of results we will get from the inquiry. Paul Tillich has constructed a massive systematic theology employing this method of "correlating" our questions with the content of revelation, and I shall employ something like his correlation method in the following.

By dwelling in the six contexts listed above, and becoming aware of the questions that arise out of them, we will be attuned to aspects of revelation that might otherwise go unnoticed. At the same time, though, our own particular way of putting questions to the sources that are believed to contain a revelatory word will cause other hidden riches in these classic sources to go unnoticed by us, and it is the merit of Barth's theology to have emphasized this point. No theology of revelation can ever be definitive, simply because we can never pose all the relevant questions for all times and circumstances. We are all limited by our particular situations. As times and situations change, our questions and concerns do also. So we can only say what revelation means for *us*, and we must not arrogantly pretend to speak for every age. Nevertheless, I think that in order for *us* to get to the substance of revelation at all we must first identify ourselves with the uncertainties and concerns that bring forth the most significant questions of our own times. For that reason we must be careful to specify in each chapter exactly what aspect of our situation we are attempting to understand. Can the idea of revelation provide the illumination we seek as we explore each aspect of our situation? Let us begin with the cosmos.

2

The Cosmos And Revelation

Who among us has not been affected, and perhaps somewhat troubled, by the dramatic new discoveries about the stars, atoms and life on earth that have taken place in this century? Because of developments in modern science our sense of the cosmos has changed rapidly and drastically, and it will continue to do so in the years ahead. We now know that we are living in a world-in-process. Our universe is "unfinished." Most scientists are convinced that the cosmos has slowly and arduously "evolved" to its present state. Over a fifteen to twenty billion year period of time, matter has struggled to become alive, and life to become conscious. What the future holds in store for this evolutionary world is impossible to say very clearly. But we can hardly help asking where it is going and whether it has any purpose to it.

The best scientific conjectures today maintain that our present universe began with a mysterious event called the "Big Bang." Then there followed an expansion of the earliest forms of matter outward into "space." This expansion took place at such a precise rate that it eventually allowed for the congealing of gases, drawn by the force of gravity, into bodies that became stars. In the intense heat at the core of these stars the lighter hydrogen atoms that had evolved much earlier were transformed into the heavier elements such as carbon, nitrogen and oxygen. This "cooking" process was of utmost importance because it produced the chemicals necessary for the evolution of planetary bodies such as our earth, and thus it made possible also the eventual appearance of life and human beings. About five billion years ago our own planet attained its orbital status around the sun. Its molten surface began to cool, and several billion years ago it acquired a solid crust upon which very primitive forms of life began to appear. These early forms of life gradually became more and more complex. Plants and animals appeared, and then, perhaps one to two million years ago, our own human species finally came onto the terrestrial scene.

Evolution does not seem to have stopped with our appearance. The universe's perpetual striving for more and more organized complexity, for increasingly intense forms of ordered novelty, continues. Our own existence here and now in the twentieth century of the Christian era is possibly still very early in the unfolding of the universe. Who can say what lies up ahead or how much further the evolution of the universe will continue? The mysterious origin from which our cosmos came and the even more mysterious future into which it is moving must render us very tentative in our attempts to say what this universe is all about. Is there anywhere a "word" that can give us some orientation? Or are we destined to remain always completely "lost in the cosmos?"

This evolutionary universe is, as far as scientific reasoning can tell, the basic context or horizon of our human existence. It is the broad "situation" out of which any educated person today addresses some of his or her most important questions about human existence. It is no longer possible for us to ignore modern cosmology and the many new and seemingly unanswerable questions it has raised. The most obvious of these questions is whether there is any final meaning to the cosmic process of which our lives seem to be such a transient and insignificant moment. Is there any purpose to the universe? This question is inseparable from our own individual concern for significance (which we shall look at in Chapter 6). For if the universe as a whole is a senseless and unintelligible movement of matter on a mindless journey toward nowhere or nothing, it would seem that our own individual claims of significance are rather tenuous also.

Of course there have always been thinkers who adopt a "tragic" interpretation of existence and who instruct us to resign ourselves to the apparent absurdity of this universe, to the cosmic indifference made even more "obvious" by the discoveries of modern science. The tragic interpretation of existence goes back to antiquity, and it has always been a powerful alternative to any "religious" vision. Its appeal lies in its ability to give the individual a sense of heroic significance in spite of the precariousness of life and the felt indifference of the universe. It insists that the universe does not care for us and that our existence does not really fit into the cosmos. But instead of collapsing in the face of this conviction the tragic vision proclaims that the final absurdity of the universe gives each of us an opportunity to exercise a courage that would not be possible if the universe were benign. By feeling in ourselves the courage of an Atlas, a Sisyphus or a Prometheus we will become convinced of our inner strength and well-being, and that will be sufficient to satisfy our private craving for significance. We do not need any "backing of the universe" to assist us in our project of achieving our self-importance.

To many intelligent people this tragic view seems to have the advantage of being "realistic" when compared to any belief in cosmic purpose. It does not need to go beyond what empirical reason can verify about the universe. The tragic, absurdist vision remains, as Albert Camus puts it, entirely "within the limits of the possible." It does not require that we imaginatively conjure up a future for our universe in which all the currently unanswered questions are finally resolved. Such "illusory" thinking is for the timid of spirit and the weak of heart. Instead the tragic view proposes that the self-esteem without which we cannot live contentedly can be gained in the face of absurdity much more readily than in the context of religious belief in universal intelligibility.

It would be rash to deny the appeal this tragic view has for us humans, all of whom are beset at times (sometimes for long periods of time) with the apparent absurdity of events and experiences. It is often much more tempting to settle for such an absurdist view than to remain steadfast in hope and trust when circumstances make the universe seem to be against us. Even within the Bible there is a strong momentary flirtation with tragic thinking, as for example, in Ecclesiastes and Job. Would it not simplify things if we would just accept the unintelligibility of the universe and not look for any "word" that might illuminate for us what it is all about?

There is another way of putting the question raised by our new cosmological sense of the vastness of the universe: is the universe alone? Have the galaxies struggled in absolutely solitary silence throughout the ages of their evolution? Has evolution been completely unaccompanied by any principle of care and concern? Has life on earth labored along for two or three billion years in lonesome struggle eventually to eke out by accident the human species which has to gather itself together in various fragile social arrangements in order to protect itself from the intolerable muteness of the universe?

Modern scientific stoicism will answer "yes" to these questions. The absolute loneliness of the universe is the basis from which all living and reflection must start. Followers of the biblical tradition, however, believe that they have heard a "word" speaking out to us in our lostness, a light shining in the darkness, a word telling us we are not alone and that through it the cosmos has been delivered from its apparent aloneness. The breaking through of this word into the apparent silence of the universe is what is called "revelation."

This word is communicated essentially in the form of a "promise." Centuries ago, according to the biblical narrative, a man who came to be known as Abraham felt the promise of a deeply fulfilling future summoning him to leave his ancestral home and launch forth into the unknown. His sons and daughters, having the same seed of hope planted in their hearts, continued the search for what had been promised to their father. The sense of a great future was passed on from generation to generation. The names of Abraham, Isaac, Jacob, Joseph, Moses, Joshua and the great judges and prophets of Israel all call to mind for believers to this day that a word of promise has broken the silence of the universe. For the Christian the person of Jesus of Nazareth constitutes the decisive breaking in of the promise of fulfillment originating with Abraham. The event of Jesus the Christ, and especially the accounts of his resurrection appearances are fundamentally *promissory* realities revealing what lies in store for the universe as a whole.[1]

---

[1] See Jürgen Moltmann, *Theology of Hope*, trans. by James W. Leitch (New York: Harper & Row, 1967), pp. 139-229.

Christians believe that in Jesus who is called the Christ God's gift of self to the universe is bestowed definitively and irreversibly. The substance of the promise made long ago is the very being of the God who planted a restlessness in the universe and a hope in the hearts of our ancestors. Revelation is the self-gift of the promising God to the universe.

But what exactly is this revelation, cosmologically speaking? In a sense we may say that it is a word of promise that relieves the universe of its aloneness. In another sense, however, the universe has never been alone. Rather it has been merely unfinished. From the moment of its creation it has "felt" the outpouring of God's own being into itself. And this divine self-donation is already a "universal" or "general" revelation. Revelation is fundamentally the self-outpouring of God into the world, arousing it to reach for further and more intense modes of fulfillment. The call of Abraham may be seen as a special instance of the breaking in of God's promise to the universe within the texture of a particular people's existence. From the point of view of cosmology the particularity of Abraham's summoning need be seen as no more scandalous than the fact that at an earlier time in cosmic evolution life itself came about at a particular place and as a unique event. By its very nature the introduction of unprecedented novelty into the cosmic process has to be a unique event. Locating the special call of Abraham in terms of cosmic evolution, and its whole series of unique moments of novel development, may help soften the scandal of particularity involved in the special call of God to a particular people to bear witness to the divine promise to the cosmos.

But what does revelation mean in terms of the evolutionary nature of the cosmos? If we look at it in the context of an evolutionary universe, revelation is the full unfolding and blossoming forth of the universe itself. It is the coming to a head of the struggles of all the cosmic ages for a significance that might validate their labored journeying. This intuition is expressed in the Letter of Paul to the Romans: "... the creation waits with eager longing for the revealing of the sons of God. We know that the whole creation has been groaning in travail together until now ..." (*Romans* 8:19,22) From one point of view revelation is the surprising and interruptive utterance of a word of promise into what otherwise is interpretable as a cosmic void. But viewed from the side of the cosmos-in-evolution it is legitimate to see revelation as the flowering fulfillment of the universe itself. Revelation is, in one sense at least, the very purpose of the evolving universe.

This theological vision might be developed as follows. In creation God gives away the fullness of divinity to the cosmos. But the cosmos in its finitude is unable to receive the boundlessness of God's self gift in one instant. Hence its response to the overflowing love is one of an ongoing expanding and enhancing the intensity of its own being in order that it might receive increasingly more of the divine life into itself. The cosmos moves and grows as a result of the implantation of the self-giving mystery that forever lies beyond it. Because of this cosmic self transcendence "time" is born. The meaning of time (which has always been a problem for philosophers) when seen in terms of God's self-revelation is that it is the mode of becoming that a world has to assume while it is receiving God into itself. The time-struck cosmos is, in other words, a world filled with promise. It cannot contain the infinite in a single moment. Therefore, it must move incrementally and indefinitely forward, receiving the fullness of the divine self-promise. This not yet completely appropriated fullness of God is called "future." And it is out of this "futurity" of the divine that the revelatory promise is issued and the cosmos lured toward its fulfillment. Evolution is the story of the world's movement into this future. As seen from the perspective of science, evolution is simply a process involving the gradual emergence of more and more complex entities and societies. But from the perspective of revelation cosmic evolution is the story of the God-of-the-future entering ever more intimately into the fabric of the universe. After an almost unimaginable number of epochs this process has reached its present status in which human beings are prominent at least in our own corner of the universe. Still the promise beckons us forward. The universe remains unfinished. And believers in revelation feel a trusting responsibility to the universe itself to allow the promise of fulfillment to lure them forward into the future. Through their trust in the future the universe continues its journey into the self-bestowing mystery of God.

The record of humankind's and the universe's response to and flight from the divine self-gift is what we call the "past." And those moments in which the world, by way of human hearers of the promissory word, has opened itself in an exceptional way to the future of God are called "revelatory." From our perspective in the "present" we look back to such moments as the basis for showing us how in the present we might face our own future. Christians find such moments narrated especially in the Bible, and they find there innumerable stories directing them to trust, now in the present, the promise of a future given ages ago but still not fully attained.

Among these stories and events the one that stands out most dramatically and normatively for Christians is the Jesus story, and within that story the narrative of his crucifixion and resurrection is all-important. We shall see later what this story might mean in terms of other contexts such as history and society. For now, though, our setting is cosmology. What is the cosmological significance of the image of the crucified and risen Jesus? In what way is it revelatory of the meaning of an evolving universe? How does it speak to the apparent silence of the epochs of evolution? Revelation, H. Richard Niebuhr has said, is the gift of an image that brings intelligibility to our world. To Christians the image of the crucified man, Jesus of Nazareth, is the central (though not the only) one through which significance and meaning is given to the world. But how would this image illuminate the meaning of the cosmic evolutionary context we are speaking of in this chapter?

Putting together some recent theological attempts to answer this question, let me offer the following interpretation. In the image of the crucified man, Jesus of Nazareth, Christians have discerned the revelation of a totally self-emptying God. The complete out-pouring (in Greek *kenosis*) of the divine life, however, is not limited to the story of this one man. The divine *kenosis*, or self-emptying, is eternally characteristic of God. It is of the divine essence to give itself completely away to the world. It does so not only in the redemptive moment of Christ's death and resurrection but also continuously in the very act of creating the world and allowing it to exist. Creation itself is the first and fundamental manifestation of the divine self-emptying.

We may understand why the creation of the cosmos already involves an act of self-humbling on God's part if we reflect briefly upon the theological notion of divine omnipotence. In order to let the world come into existence, and then to continue to be itself and not just an emanation of God's own being, an omnipotent Creator would somehow have to restrain or "rein in" the divine presence and power. Divine creativity would have to "contract itself" away from any compulsive "control" over things in order that the world might come forth in genuine otherness in relation to God. Creation then would not be so much an act of divine self-expansion as it would be the result of God's self-withdrawal. It would be the result of a divine "self-contraction." Divine power would be manifest in "weakness" as St. Paul says. In the image of the crucified man, Jesus the Christ, the Christian may see the historical revelation of this self-sacrificing God out of whose absolute generosity the world is allowed to be.

Viewed in the light of this kenotic image, a view available only to faith of course, the evolution of the cosmos is given an intelligibility that it would not otherwise have. The apparent randomness as well as the struggling and unpredictable meanderings that science sees in evolution, and which have caused so much theological controversy, are just what we should expect if the world is in some way left to be itself by the non-interfering goodness of a self-emptying God. The indeterminacy that science has found at the levels of matter (uncertainty), life (chance mutations), and human existence (freedom) are essential cosmological ingredients if the autonomy of the world is not to collapse into the being of the Creator-God (in which case it would no longer be a world distinct unto itself). The possibility of its wandering away from what God intends for it is an inevitable risk in any universe where the cosmos is given its own genuine, autonomous existence. In order for the world to have its own existence, its Creator would in some way have to be "absent" to that world. And precisely by restraining its "omnipotence" (a notion suggested by Simone Weil, Geddes MacGregor, Jürgen Moltmann, Nicholai Berdyaev and many others) the creative principle would be simultaneously giving itself away to that created world. In speaking of the creation of the world we have to abandon our crude notions of mechanical causation, and in doing so we can remove a number of unnecessary theological problems that have resulted from the misleading identification of creation with efficient causation. The image of the crucified, therefore, allows faith to understand the evolving universe as the effect of God's kenotic self-revelation.

The image of the "crucified God" also makes it clear to faith that the sufferings of the world and its evolutionary struggle are not solitary and ultimately unredeemable. For they are forever being taken into the very life of God where, according to the many biblical images of "resurrection," they are transformed into a new creation. This, at any rate, is how the cosmic process might be seen when it is regarded through the central images of Christian revelation.

But can this revelation be proven? Is it reasonable? Can it stand up to the critical questions that will inevitably come from the "enlightened" modern mind? I shall address these questions focally in Chapter 7, but let me state now why it is that revelation seems to elude the grasp of what we ordinarily call reason. I think we can explain why this is so especially in the context of our picture of an evolving world.

As the world has evolved, new and richer forms of existence have gradually appeared. We may, somewhat simplistically, speak of four successively higher or "emergent" levels that have evolved: matter, plant life, animal life, human life. As we move up this ladder of emergence each higher level includes considerably more of what may be called "mentality" or "feeling." Matter seems to possess only a negligible amount of "mentality" or "feeling" (though some philosophers insist that sub-atomic events are also actually constituted by their "feeling" the fields of force surrounding them). Plant life obviously possesses a deeper and wider sentience than does mere matter. Animals are characterized by an even deeper form of "awareness." And, finally, human life goes a qualitative leap further in its capacity not only for deep feeling and awareness, but also for self-awareness. Therefore, if we use as our axis of measurement the emergence and expansion of "mentality," we can maintain that there has indeed been a certain "directionality" in evolution.

Notice that each higher "level" in this emergent process

includes the levels that lie beneath it, but it cannot be fully explained in terms of the lower levels. For example, life includes matter, but the sciences such as chemistry and physics that deal with matter are incapable on their own of explaining all that is involved in life. And the human mind includes life and matter, but it cannot be fully understood in terms of chemistry and biology. Something qualitatively new and irreducible has been added at each emergent level.[2]

Now it is entirely possible, as I have said earlier, that the appearance of the human species with its peculiar form of consciousness is by no means the end of evolution. In fact it is more likely that evolution can continue indefinitely (within the parameters established by the laws of thermodynamics), and for all we know, the present moment may still be very early in the full unfolding of the universe. If hydrogen atoms, which were once the dominant "species" of being in the universe, had been conscious they may easily have conjectured that they were the final product of the evolutionary process. However, they left themselves open to being patterned and transformed into "higher" types of entities. And each succeeding level has "left itself open" to being informed and patterned by yet higher entities. An obvious illustration of this recurrent phenomenon is the manner in which invariant chemical processes of nature leave themselves open to being taken up into living cells, or the way in which cells allow themselves to be patterned into more and more complex living and conscious processes.

It is also entirely consistent with the patterns we notice in cosmic emergence for us to maintain that the human sphere of mentality is now being invited by the "forces of evolution" to leave itself open to an informing and patterning by a yet higher and more "conscious" level. Why should we assume that human consciousness is not so invited when every previous level has found its fulfillment only by being taken up into a higher dimension? What I am calling "revelation," therefore, may be *cosmologically* located as a further development in the universe's evolution of consciousness. And as we would expect, revelation would be no more reducible to reason or

---

[2]For a more extensive discussion of these points see my book on science and religion, *The Cosmic Adventure* (New York: Paulist Press, 1984), pp. 48-74.

ordinary consciousness than life is to matter. Revelation is no more understandable in the categories of the "enlightened mind" of reason than life is explainable in terms of chemistry. Therefore, the reason why revelation is so elusive to our ordinary human rational processes is precisely because it fits so securely into the emergent evolutionary scheme of things. According to this vision a higher level can include or comprehend a lower, but a lower cannot include or comprehend a higher. If revelation occurs at a higher emergent level than human reason, then we should not be surprised that it remains at least somewhat out of reason's grasp.

Some contemporary theologians are suggesting that, from the point of view of evolutionary cosmology, reason, like the lower levels that preceded its appearance in the universe, must leave itself open to being taken up into the "higher dimension" of revelation. Revelation, therefore, is the evolutionary fulfillment of reason, in no way reducible to the latter. And just as life does not contradict chemistry, or human reason does not contradict the biotic processes in which it dwells, so revelation cannot contradict reason. It dwells in reason and utilizes our ordinary rational faculties, but at the same time it "transcends" the rational level of cosmic evolution.[3]

Conclusion

I have not yet specified in detail the content of what I am calling revelation. I shall begin to do so in the following chapter where our starting point will be history rather than cosmology. My objective in this chapter has been simply to state how a possible revelation may be situated in terms of the very broad context of cosmic evolution. I would like now to add one final point concerning the cosmic location of "faith" in terms of the emergent, evolutionary universe. The attitude which human consciousness must assume in order to accept the promissory essence of revelation is a simple trust or confidence that we usually refer to as "faith." Faith is not an act

[3]These ideas have been developed in different ways by Teilhard de Chardin and process theology. I have summarized these ideas in *The Cosmic Adventure*.

of blind credulity or the acceptance of irrational and absurd ideas. Rather it is the commitment of one's whole existence to a promissory word. It is an act of entrusting oneself to a pattern of existence that is present in promise and which reason cannot get itself around comprehensively. In short, faith, when viewed from the point of view of cosmology, may be defined as the act or state of leaving our human consciousness open to being patterned by a higher emergent dimension whose substance always remains beyond our comprehension. It is the allowing of our human existence to be taken up into a cosmic story whose final meaning is promised but not yet clear.

We can have only a fragmentary and opaque glimpse of the final meaning of the universe. And this partial view is given to faith first of all through "images" that accompany the promise given to us in the medium of history. We turn now to an examination of the *historical* situation through which God's revelatory self-gift to the world is mediated.

3

History and Revelation

We live not only in nature but also in history. History, in the broadest meaning of the term, is the total sequence of events that have occurred in the universe. Thus we can speak with cosmologists about the "history of the universe" or the "history of evolution." In a stricter sense of the term, however, history is the chronicle of specifically *human* events that have taken place. While we humans share much with the animals, there is something that sets us somewhat apart from nature. This is especially our existence in history.

The distinction of history from nature is logically possible because of the existence of human freedom. Whereas nature appears for the most part to be a realm of relatively predictable and largely causal occurrences, human existence is characterized by a freedom that we do not find, in any but an analogous sense, in nature. Human existence therefore is said to "transcend" nature in that it has a dimension of personal freedom that is not easily understood in terms of the sciences that deal with nature. Though there are "social" or human sciences that attempt to go as far as they can in achieving a scientific understanding of human activity, there is always a residue of the human that eludes scientific prediction, namely, our freedom. Thus, because of our freedom we may think of history as a second aspect of our situation, quite distinct (though, of course, not separate) from cosmology.

Revelation of History

Because history is made up cumulatively of the actions and experiences of persons endowed with the elusive quality of freedom, its intelligibility is not easily comprehended, that is, if it has any intelligibility at all. The search for a possible meaning to history has been one of the most frustrating, though fascinating, enterprises undertaken ever since we first became aware that we do not live in nature in the same way that other species do. Once we acquired the distinct feeling that our historical existence has "exiled" us to some degree from the regularities and rhythms of nature, we became restless to find exactly where we do fit in. What pattern or order, if any, does history have that can give us a sure sense of where we are situated, of what our origins, destinies and identities are? The "fall" of the human species from the predictabilities of nature into the turmoil of history has been a most adventurous development in the total unfolding of the universe. But it has certainly been a troubling one as well, and we are far from having a firm hold on its significance in terms of the entire sweep of things.

Because the movement into history has been a tumultuous and even terrifying occurrence for our species, there has always been a strong temptation to return to the womb of nature. There seems to lie in nature's regularities a haven from the open-endedness and unpredictability of living in history. Yet from antiquity to modern existentialism we find warnings that such a "gnostic" move away from our historicity is regressive, that it is a backward retreat which conflicts with authentic human existence. The move into history is irreversible, even though much suffering and uncertainty will inevitably beset those who have ventured into it.

Interestingly, biblical religion itself has been responsible to a great extent for sparking the disturbing impulse to move beyond a purely natural existence and into the uncertainty of history. In fact, it seems accurate to say that biblical ways of thinking opened the horizon of "history" to humankind in an unprecedented and decisive way. Biblical religion did so especially because of the promissory nature of its revelation. In God's revelatory gift of the divine self to human consciousness in the form of *promise*, the horizon of the future began to appear more obvious, and with its beckoning promise our biblical ancestors moved decisively into history as the central context of their lives and aspirations.

Therefore, instead of our speaking only of God's revelation *in* history, it is just as appropriate for us to speak here in terms of God's revelation *of* history. History is the content , and not just the medium of revelation. History is itself what is revealed or "unveiled." History as such is the horizon of unpredictability and novelty opened up to us by a revelatory promise.

The emergence of the Hebrew religion then was a very unsettling occurrence, and we are still reeling from its appearance. In the call of Abraham to leave the home of his ancestors, in Moses' leading his people away from acquiescence in Egyptian slavery, in the prophetic protests against any localizing or naturalizing domestication of Yahweh's presence, in the apocalyptic rebellions against the status quo, in Jesus' idealizing of homelessness, in the Evangelists' turning our attention toward the Risen Lord and in St. Paul's relentless call to freedom from the slavery of legalism, we have a constant chorus of discontent at the idea that we can find our fulfillment in what nature apart from history has given us. Our fulfillment as human beings begins by our embarking upon a journey into the unknown future opened up by the revelatory promise that pulls us away from the familiarity of a purely natural existence. This call into history has been troubling as well as promising, and it is always tempting to turn back toward the "paradise" of non-historical existence.

The human transition from nature into history has brought us at least part way out of the ancient enclosure in cycles of seasons. It has pointed us into a future that is more than just a return to the sameness of the past. Novelty and surprise are essential to the future out of which history is born. There is no turning back to the predictable and reversible, much as we are inclined at times to move in that direction. History, unlike nature as such, is apparently open-ended and irreversible. Although there is a certain sense in which "history repeats itself," events in the historical arena are never recurrent with the same regularity and predictability as are natural occurrences. They lead us into an indefiniteness which we often tend to domesticate by using analogies from predictable natural occurrences, such as "cycles" or "spirals." But in the end, the outcome of history eludes the controlling attempts of our sciences, and we are confronted with nothing less than a mystery of indefinite openness. We refer to this mystery as the "future" and the appropriate response to it as "hope."

The uncertainty of the future into which history is taking us might be unbearable unless some beacon up ahead lights our way and guides us through the fog toward some vision of fulfillment. The quest for revelation may therefore be understood, in the present context at least, as the quest for some resolution of the mistiness that confronts us as we peer into the unknown outcome of historical events. We are so immersed in the contemporary stream of happenings that we have little idea of the geography through which the historical current that bears us along may be flowing. Human beings existing in history have always longed for a perspective that would assure them that the present is not unrelated to a meaningful future. And so we may understand the "revelation" we are looking for as the unfolding of this future, the disclosure to us within the limits of our historical situation of a wider pattern of significance that bestows on the present and the past an intelligibility that would otherwise not be evident.

But is there indeed such a disclosure? Has such a pattern been laid out before us? Can we confidently discern any meaning in history? Such pattern or meaning is certainly not obvious to everyone. Most intellectuals today are skeptical of any talk about the meaning of history. They are aware as never before of the "historically contingent" nature of all human consciousness, that is, of how even the most apparently objective knowledge is conditioned and relativized by the context out of which it is nurtured. We are all immersed in the relativities of our own cultures, and therefore we do not have any vantage point that would allow us to state what truth is in any universal sense. Hence no matter what our thoughts may be regarding the meaning of history, they will inevitably appear questionable to others who simply do not "see" what we see in history.

Nevertheless, the substance of biblical faith allows us to say, at the very least, the following: without a trust in the promise of a meaningful and unimaginably fulfilling future, the move into history would be intolerable. History without promise is unbearable. It is no wonder that so many avenues of escape are devised by those who find a history without promise so utterly terrifying today. Gnostic movements of the body, the spirit and the mind are inevitable temptations whenever history is exorcised of its promise, the expectancy of fulfillment that brought it about in the first place. The romantic retreat into an "unadulterated" and uncivilized nature, the resurgence of barbarism, the escape into drugs, alcohol, depersonalized sex—these and many other exits are at least partially explainable as a result of the feeling that nothing will come of involving ourselves in historical existence. Such escapist movements are quite intelligible whenever history is seen as bereft of a fulfilling future.

Parallel escapes from history are being entertained in the intellectual world today. For example, some important philosophical and literary movements give sophisticated and learned expression to the modern despair about a possible meaning and promise to history. Interestingly, though, many of these learned movements of escape from history still manifest a deep hunger for a better world than the one to which history seems to have brought us. The reaching out for a better and fuller world of promise is never completely quenched. Hoping, in some mode or other, is a part of our nature, a "prototypical human gesture."[1] Today, however, this longing for something more satisfying is often exercised by reaching for some sort of "fulfillment" apart from history.

Biblical revelation refuses to let us despair of history. The idea of revelation is inseparable from a promise that our movement into history is not in vain. Revelation therefore may be understood as the promise of an ultimate meaning to history (symbolized in the Bible especially by the notion of the "kingdom of God)." It does not specify in any completely clear way what this meaning is. The meaning of history as far as we are concerned at this moment, consists of the promise it holds

---

[1]See Peter Berger, *A Rumor of Angels* (Garden City, New York: Doubleday Anchor Books, 1970), pp. 49-75.

of ultimate justice and freedom, of a fulfillment beyond our expectations. At the same time history may also be understood as itself essentially a product of revelation. History is constituted as such by God's gift of a future that pulls us out of the safety of nature and into a mysterious openness accessible only to hope. Only by our opening ourselves in hope can the promise take root in our world and continue to keep the horizon of history open for us. Revelation *is* promise, and without our response of hope neither revelation nor history can become an actuality. It is quite understandable, then, that whenever human hope fails and despair about the future grows, there is often a resurgence of attempts to find refuge in either hedonistic or ascetic flights from history.

Revelation means the disclosing to us of a new forum for our existing, namely, the sphere of a promise of fulfillment that makes history possible. In relating ourselves to the promise given to Abraham (who stands to Jews, Muslims and Christians alike as "our father in faith"), and by observing the partial fulfillment of this promise in surprising ways time without number, we sense that we have been given a new context, beyond the purely natural, within which to dwell. And through this gift of history the cosmos has been given a future far surpassing the repetitions, regularities and rhythms of nature alone.

In Christianity the season of Advent celebrates in a heightened way the ages-old sense that an infinite and inexhaustible divine care seeks continually to renew our lives and move us out into the realm of history's promise. The liturgies of this season of promise are filled with biblical images of trust in God's power to bring new hope where there was previously only a sense of utter impossibility. One of the most moving is from the book of Isaiah (11, 1; 6-9), where it is promised that out of the lifeless "stump" of Jesse will come forth a shoot symbolizing God's promise-keeping fidelity at a time of historical hopelessness. Following from this blossoming of new life impossible, incongruous occurrences are to be expected—wolves living in harmony with lambs, children playing with snakes. For reasons of space I cannot quote extensively from the Scriptures in this book, but the reader is encouraged to read and dwell within the countless similar passages where the impossible breaks into and renews history, always by being received in hope. It is difficult to read very far in the Bible without concluding that its essential meaning is that we may trust in the impossible, and that the realm of the purely predictabe is far from exhausting the limits of reality. The following passage, written at a time when it would have been quite "realistic" to despair of Israel's future, may serve to exemplify the trust to which the revelatory promise calls us, not least in situations of utter desperation:

> There shall come forth a shoot from the stump of Jesse,
> and a branch shall grow out of its roots.
> And the Spirit of the Lord shall rest upon him. . .
>
> Righteousness shall be the girdle of his waist,
> and faithfulness the girdle of his loins.
> The wolf shall dwell with the lamb,
> and the leopard shall lie down with the kid,
> and the calf and the lion and the fatling together,
> and a little child shall lead them. (Isaiah 11:1; 5-7)

Revelation in History

However, we must have some grounds for believing in such promises of an ultimately fulfilling and "impossible" future. Without such a basis we will inevitably be tempted to join the caravans of those who have decided to forsake history for more immediate but less fulfilling satisfactions. Faith can never be completely without reasons. It must have a foundation based in human experience itself. Revelation, if it is to be accepted, must not only give us a promise. It must also provide some evidence that there is a principle of fidelity operative throughout our history. In other words it must consist of concrete deeds and events in our history that vindicate our hope for fulfillment.

It is in this connection that we may speak more strictly of revelation *in* history. For as we look with our tradition into the past we can discern innumerable instances of God's fidelity to the promise that is revelation. This fidelity is embodied paradigmatically in the account of the *covenant* of Yahweh with Israel, when God is portrayed as pledging everlasting care and companionship and asks only that we, the people of the covenant, keep our side of the agreement by mediating the divine goodness and justice to all (Exodus 19-24). The theme of divine fidelity is undoubtedly the dominant theme in biblical religion, and all we have to do is look into our own history as a people to observe how it has been repeatedly and continuously manifested. Our traditions and Scriptures embody accounts of the instances when God's fidelity to the covenant appears time and again in the face of our own infidelity. God's revelation in history, from creation to the hoped-for Parousia, is the story of the mighty acts of a God whose essence is always fidelity and promise-keeping in spite of our own lack of trust. Our history is comprised essentially of events in which faith sees the presence of a God whose passionate concern for the integrity and happiness of human life is unfailing. For Christians, of course, the Christ-event is the decisive manifestation of the divine promise and fidelity.

Discernment of this and other revelatory events requires that we belong to the inner life of a faith community that perceives its very identity as having been founded by the story of divine acts of fidelity to the promise. To those who participate in this "inner history" such occurrences as the call of Abraham, the Exodus from Egypt, the tortured lives of the prophets, the redemption of Israel and Judah from captivity, the events surrounding the life and death of Jesus, including the acts of the apostles and the establishment of the Church, all have a promissory significance that would not inevitably be obvious to scientific historians. Partaking of the internal memory of a people and its own story gives us a perspective on these strange occurrences that would hardly be arrived at by way of a detached, objective or external chronicling of these same events through the methods of a scientific historian. Our conviction that we belong to a history whose meaning is promise could hardly take shape outside the life of a community whose very existence is based on that promise.

H. Richard Niebuhr, more clearly than any other modern theologian, has articulated the difference between internal and external history and its importance for understanding the idea of revelation. Though his distinction should not be stretched too far, it is quite useful at least as a starting point for understanding the meaning of revelation in history. Niebuhr gives us a simple analogy to help us comprehend the duality of internal and external history. Consider the case of a blind man who undergoes an operation and, as a result, receives back his sight. Then try to imagine how his own account of this momentous healing event would differ from that of the doctors who performed the operation. The account of the latter will be framed in the detached, clinical language of medical science, in the idiom of a decidedly external reporting. On the other hand, the account of the blind man cannot be clinically "objective" but will be filled with language of deep feeling, gratitude and emotional involvement. It will be an "inner history," giving us a perspective which the doctors who performed the operation are not in a position to provide. Both the external and internal accounts are valid, but they cannot be reduced to or evaluated in terms of the standards pertaining to each other's approaches to the same event. And the inner history provided by the man whose sight has been restored will give us an intimacy with the event that even the most careful clinical language could never come close to providing.

Similarly the revelatory significance of the promissory events in the life of Israel and the Church will not be obvious from the perspective of a purely external accounting. An external report cannot state exactly why we may perceive these events as a basis for our hope here and now. Scientific history can shed much interesting light on the historical circumstances surrounding the great events upon which our hope is founded, and critical historical work can even become a necessary and corrective ingredient in a community's recalling of its foundational moments. But only a participation in the "inner life" of a community puts us in a position to experience and confess these events as moments of divine fidelity to the covenantal promises that comprise God's relation to our life as a people founded upon these events. To grasp the reality of a possible revelation in history, we must be prepared to risk involvement in the life of a community established by this memory of an internal history often inaccessible to "objective" recording.[2]

---

[2]This distinction of internal from external history is not intended, though, to make history outside of our own tradition irrelevant. In actuality there is only one history, and the revelatory promise perceived in internal history is intended to bring all of history to its fulfillment. For the above discussion of internal and external history see H. Richard Niebuhr, *The Meaning of Revelation*, pp. 44 ff.

Revelation and the Future

In biblical religion we are given innumerable accounts of God's address to Israel and to the Christian community. But in these accounts there is no complete disclosure of God or of history's meaning. Instead there is typically an exhortation to look forward into the future. The theophanies (manifestations of God) in the Bible are predominantly promissory appearances of God pointing toward a dimension of the yet-to-come. There is the withholding of a future except in promise, a future that can only be approached through a posture called hope. Even in Jesus' resurrection appearances, when viewed against the backdrop of the Old Testament theophanies, as Jürgen Moltmann has written, the first Christians experienced a Christ who still has a future and who invites them and us to share the promise of his personal future with him. For that reason there can be no adequate faith in the Resurrection without a deep hope here and now for the future of our own historical existence as tied up with the future of Christ and the whole of human history. The Christ who comes to Christians in the Eucharistic celebration of the memory of his death and resurrection is one who is yet to come. The promise of Christ's and the world's future pervades the Christian notion of revelation.[3]

It is precisely the *promissory* nature of revelation that I wish to accentuate here. If we are to avoid the inevitable accusation of being overly hasty in our judgments about the meaning of history we must admit that things do not yet make complete sense to us in any clear way. Believers in revelation are not in a position to say exactly what the meaning of history is. What has been revealed to them is not complete clarity but a promise that demands trust.

However, to Christian faith this promise is more than enough. To faith the promise of a still undisclosed future is all we need to light up our history and to give us consolation in the face of the apparent absurdities that have taken place within the course of human events. The revelatory promise of Yahweh, first bestowed on Abraham and handed down

---

[3] Moltmann, *Theology of Hope*, passim.

through the precious centuries of Jewish and Christian history, is in fact all that we would be capable of grasping at this juncture of time. It is only the promissory nature of revelation that can deliver it from the countless trivializations of human hope that have poisoned our human history with premature portraits of history's meaning. Our understandable human impatience for meaningful fulfillment has led us time and again to imagine that a particular conception of social order is the ultimate stage in history's movement. Innumerable atrocities have been committed against those who have not accommodated themselves to the many "visions" of human existence that have been proposed. But it is the very nature of "promise" that we learn to *wait*, ideally in joyful expectation, but nonetheless, wait. It might seem that such waiting puts us at a disadvantage in comparison with those who want to possess. But this is not the case. As Paul Tillich says, we are stronger when we wait than when we possess.

> The condition of man's relation to God is first of all one of *not* having, *not* seeing, *not* knowing, and *not* grasping. A religion in which that is forgotten, no matter how ecstatic or active or reasonable, replaces God by its own creation of an image of God.... It is not easy to endure this not having God, this waiting for God.... For how can God be possessed? Is God a thing that can be grasped and known among other things? Is God less than a human person? We always have to wait for a human being. Even in the most intimate communion among human beings, there is an element of *not* having and *not* knowing, and of waiting. Therefore, since God is infinitely hidden, free, and incalculable, we must wait for Him in the most absolute and radical way. He is God for us just in so far as we do *not* possess Him.... We have God through *not* having Him.[4]

Radical waiting is of course often a most difficult and ungratifying response to life. But it is also the most realistic, fulfilling and empowering:

---

[4]Paul Tillich, *The Shaking of the Foundations* (New York: Charles Scribner's Sons, 1948), p. 55.

If we wait in hope and patience, the power of that for which we wait is already effective within us. He who waits in absolute seriousness is already grasped by that for which he waits. He who waits in patience has already received the power of that for which he waits. He who waits passionately is already an active power himself, the greatest power of transformation in personal and historical life. We are stronger when we wait than when we possess.[5]

It is important to observe, in this connection, that the sense of the breaking in of a revelatory promise has always been most intense among the poor and the oppressed, among those who have to wait and are most distant from any possessing. Their poverty has given them a vulnerability that opens them to the future in an exceptional way. And that is why these people have been the bearers of revelation's promise. It is not the possessive and the powerful but the childlike, the weak and the disenfranchised through whom history's meaning has been most fully mediated. The Bible is filled with stories illustrating this motif. Especially those who are not in possession of their lives, those who have to wait, have been the most open to receiving the Good News of history's promise.[6]

---

[5]*Ibid.*, p. 151.

[6]Today in our situation "after Auschwitz" we need to rethink the idea of revelation in terms of theological questions raised by the unspeakable horror of the so-called "Holocaust" and other massive murderings of our century. Such necessary rethinking is beyond the scope of this brief introduction, but the theme of "forgotten suffering" taken up in the following chapter would perhaps be a starting point.

4

Society and Revelation

History is usually written by the conquerors. It is hardly surprising then that written history often suppresses the memory of the suffering inflicted upon the millions of individuals abandoned in history's wake. And yet such suffering is a major part of the objective content of history. Viewed from a certain perspective history seems to be, as Hegel puts it, a "butcher's bench." It is apparently anything but a divine gift made possible by the promise of fulfillment. The experimentation with social, political and economic structures necessitated by the move into historical existence has produced prolonged sufferings in spite of the best intentions. And often the most entrancing visions of social idealism have been accompanied, especially in modern times, by the annihilation of millions of individuals who do not seem to have fit into the plans of the new societies. We need to look only at the massive murderings prompted by Nazism, the Stalinist regime and more recently by the Khmer Rouge in Cambodia for some obvious examples. No account of God's revelation in history can leave out the largely unrecorded chronicle of neglect, mutilation and slaughter that have taken place behind the scene of publicly accessible events. No conception of meaning in history can have validity unless it takes into account the "dangerous" memory of the forgotten sufferings that constitute so much of the substance of history. Yet how many philosophies or theologies of history have actually accomplished such a redemption of forgotten suffering? We have a few sensitive film-makers, journalists and novelists to thank for not allowing us to forget completely some of the atrocities hidden from the front pages. But our theologies have too often forgotten this suffering. So now, especially in a theology of revelation, we must make a special place for the memory of suffering.

This hidden suffering has resulted partly from natural disasters that lie beyond human control. But for the most part it has been the consequence of the ways in which humans have organized or attempted to organize their social existence. Political, social and economic patterns have determined a large part of the lives of all peoples. The *social* context of our existence is therefore a major aspect of the situation out of which we look for some revelatory "answer" to our quest for the optimal "order" by which to enhance the quality of human existence.

The impulse to establish social order is itself motivated by assumptions as to what constitutes good order or the "good life." Value judgments and ethical preoccupations motivate societal planning, and it is under the guise of the search for order and "the good" that societies with their political and economic components are established. Well-meaning and self-sacrificing devotees of great visions, together with fanatics and opportunists, collaborate to produce our societies and to preserve them in the face of the chaos that continues to threaten them. In order to prevent the possibility of subversion they deem it essential at times to torture and even eliminate those individuals who do not fit into the social plans or who raise critical questions about the planned or established regimes. Often the exceptionally imaginative and creative people are the ones most vulnerable to persecution, since through them even newer and more disturbing dreams of a still better world enter the arena of our social consciousness, stirring up criticism of the present order and making obsolete our plans for a new society.

When we look honestly at history and reflect on the poignant human struggles for an acceptable social order we might be easily tempted to cynicism. (And today, on the brink of potential nuclear annihilation, such cynicism may even seem to be the most realistic attitude to take toward our social and political existence). For we are caught on the horns of an apparently irresolvable dilemma. It seems that if people settle for the social, political and economic status quo, they are usually ignoring the needs of those who are put at a disadvantage by the present order. For example, societies based on slavery have at times been relatively stable and prosperous, but at what price to the slaves? Or a society in which a certain percentage of people will be "inevitably" unemployed may seem to be the only plausible economic order; but what about the needs of the unemployed? On the other hand, if people envisage social reforms to take care of the needy and marginalized, history shows us that the actual implementation of these enticing social visions has also led to massive sufferings for other innocent people. Every major revolution has had this consequence. Is there any way to avoid this dilemma? Or is there any resolution of it? Is it even possible to have a social order that is not only an order, but also a *just* social order? And is it possible to bring about reforms, or to plan a better economy, without causing even more suffering?

Reflection on the "impossible" situation of creating the right social and economic configurations has led us to the point where we may be open to a "solution" that lies, in part at least, beyond our own powers of planning. The fact of revelation (in all six of our contexts) becomes evident to faith especially in those situations which, according to human reckoning, are characterized by what we may call "impossibility." Its proximity to situations of what we usually take to be impossibility has characterized the biblical promise from the very beginning of the story of Yahweh's involvement with people of the covenant. So when we think of the notion of revelation today, it is important that we continue to understand it in terms of the divine promise of a way out of dilemmas that seem resistant to any possible solution we can imagine. An attitude of trust in God's fidelity must accompany our understanding of the seemingly irredeemable socio-economic quandaries we find ourselves in today. (And we might emphasize here also the "impossible" task of bringing about any resolution of the nuclear arms race and what seems to many reasonable people the "inevitable" extinction of human life if the momentum continues according to the "logic" inherent in present international politics).

It is doubtful that revelation in its essentially surprising and unpredictable newness could be experienced decisively except in such situations of apparent impossibility. And it is quite a simple matter to become aware of the "impossible" dead-ends to which our human attempts to establish the "right" social order on the basis of our own purely human ideals have always led us. When we realize the frustration to which our best intentioned social preoccupations bring us, we are perhaps once again in a position to hearken to a revelatory response to our situation.

If we are looking for a *specific* answer to our social quest, however, we will not find it in revelation. The revelatory "answer " will inevitably be quite disappointing to us if we expect it to fall within the general class of "solutions" that have been proposed by social, political and economic experts. In our obsession with finding the definitive social solution we can easily end up trivializing the biblical response to our quest, that is, if we scour the texts for a specific social program. The biblical response cannot be so easily diluted. Without doing it great violence we cannot look into the Bible for *the* perfect answer to our own socio-economic problems. Such a fundamentalism is unworthy of any genuine faith in revelation. For the revelatory response lies on a different plane from the one shaped by our usual social expectations and planning. It is once again only in the sphere of hope and promise that we may authentically seek a response to the unfairness and suffering (including the forgotten suffering) inflicted by social structures. And it is only in the sphere of hope and promise that we may find the "answer" to the most significant threat ever experienced by humans, that of nuclear annihilation. In the biblical tradition such hope and promise are embodied especially in the symbolism of the "Kingdom of God."

Revelation and the Kingdom of God

In the Bible, the theme of the "Kingdom of God" is the one that stands out most obviously as the goal of our social searching. From the perspective of the social dimension of our situation we may understand the quest for revelation in terms of the long human quest for the Kingdom of God. The precise meaning of the Kingdom is still being investigated by biblical scholars, but we can confidently say that its significance is at least partially grasped in terms of two other prominent biblical themes: *justice* and *liberation*. These themes become more and more transparent as we move through Israel's history into the mind of Jesus and the early Christian Church. John Donahue has characterized the biblical ideal of justice (*sedaqah*) by calling it "fidelity to the demands of a relationship."

> The justice of Yahweh is . . . his saving power, his fidelity to his role of Lord of the covenant. It is also his indictment of sin and his call to return or conversion. Justice represents a victory over powers which threaten the destruction of the world. It is manifest both in the historical life of people and as an object of their eschatological hope. . . . concern for the defenseless in society is not a command designed simply to promote social harmony, but is rooted in the nature of Yahweh himself who is defender of the oppressed. . . . The doing of justice is not the application of religious faith, but its substance; without it, God remains unknown.[1]

It is clear from this brief summary of the biblical vision that justice is a *revelatory* aspect of our social relationships and that without it the God of revelation remains hidden from us. Our own practice of justice, which inevitably includes careful social programs and planning for the needs of the poor, is a necessary condition for God's becoming manifest in our historical and social existence. For us to experience today the revelation of God we must also experience and practice justice in the social dimension of our existence. To the extent that justice does not yet reign, revelation is still obscured. It may be that the difficulty we have believing in divine revelation is the effect of our being so jaded by the injustice that often seems to prevail.

---

[1]John R. Donahue, S.J. "Biblical Perspectives on Justice," In John C. Haughey, ed., *The Faith that Does Justice* (New York: Paulist Press, 1977), pp. 69-76, *passim*.

At heart the apparent "implausibility" of the idea of revelation to modernity with its secularistic assumptions, is less the result of its "unscientific" appearance than the consequence of the untransformed status of our unjust social structures.

And yet, the revelation of God's justice has, at least to faith, made an irreversible entrance into our world. It is present in the mode of promise, and it is deeply entrenched wherever there is hope. This hope, however, it not content with passive or quietistic complacency anymore than it is impatient with the absence of immediate achievement of social utopias. It is an active hope, energized by the conviction of an irretractable promise. And that means it is a transformative hope, intent to alter those social structures that impede the pouring out of God's justice here and now. Such a hope has to be involved with social planning, though with the constant provision that our human plans are likely to be short-sighted, onesided and in need of the judgment by a wider vision of justice. Social planning is not to be repudiated as such. The biblical ideal of justice requires only that we avoid a planning that does not provide for the poor and that forgets about the sufferings of the past. The social planning of the present century has been vitiated especially by its neglect of the poor, the disenfranchised, the helpless, the stranger and of forgotten sufferings of the past, of all those elements that do not "fit." But any social vision that leaves these out is destined to be only a fragment. The Kingdom of God is an image of social fulfillment that challenges us to widen our own social understanding so as to include all of these, even when it does not seem economically feasible. Its very comprehensiveness, of course, makes it seem unbelievable from the perspective of our customary styles of social planning. Yet the biblical promise demands nothing less than the widening of our social visions and our sense of justice so as to include all those elements that we normally suppress.

Another aspect of the Kingdom of God is the theme of liberation. Intimately associated with "justice," the theme of liberation is central to the biblical vision of God and of society. The Exodus event, the liberation of an oppressed people from the threats of slavery and annihilation, is the central event through which Israel came to understand the nature of God. It is not possible, therefore, in the biblical context at least, to think of God without simultaneously thinking of liberation. Loving and liberating justice is God's essence, and it is out of this essence that the revelatory promise is given to society and its history. In the biblical context this liberating justice does not refer only to a salvation beyond history, but also to a salvation of history as well as a deliverance within history. As I mentioned earlier, the promise of deliverance is felt first and becomes most intensely alive in the situations of those whom our social institutions have marginalized and made to feel as though they do not belong. It is to such as these that Jesus' proclamation of the Good News of freedom and justice was delivered first and foremost. Social outcasts, trodden and rejected people have been the constant mediators of revelation. For it is through their hope in and acceptance of a promise of liberation that a space was opened up for our own history and future to make its appearance. The debt we owe to the poor for allowing the promise of liberation to enter into the sphere of history is inestimable.

For centuries Christian theology has been able to hide from the themes of promise, justice and liberation that permeate the biblical texts. An over-emphasis on the metaphysical aspects of God as understood especially in terms of Greek philosophy has sometimes concealed and domesticated the liberating themes in the Bible and their transformative implications for our social, political and economic life here and now. But it is no longer possible to suppress these themes, and particularly in any attempt to get to the heart of what is meant by revelation. In the context of our social situation, revelation means the promise of justice for and liberation of the oppressed and the poor, of all whose basic needs have not been met and whose human dignity has not been recognized. And encounter with the God of revelation takes place primarily in those situations through which the sense of a promise of liberating justice breaks through into our history. Do we have to look far to find such situations today?

The Kingdom of God is an image pointing to a fulfillment of our social existence in a justice and freedom that can never be fully implemented by human planning alone, though of course human planning is not excluded. Just as God's creation of the universe is not opposed to, but requires, our own creativity, so also the establishment of the Kingdom of God requires our own active complicity. Our own involvement takes the form especially of our "practicing"justice and liberation in a spirit of hope that the promised reign of justice and freedom is not a vain dream but a realistic possibility. More concretely this involvement begins with our own concern for bringing justice to those who need it most, the poor. But the "Kingdom of God" is essentially God's creation of justice and freedom in a way that goes far beyond anything we could dream of for ourselves.

Awareness of the coming Kingdom of God seems to have been most intense among the poor and oppressed who have been helpless to do anything about their suffering themselves except to call upon God out of the desperateness of their situation. A sense of the promissory revelation of God has entered our history by way of the poor, the weak, the wandering homeless and the suffering. We cannot overlook this simple aspect of biblical religion when we try to understand the meaning of God's revelation in terms of our own socio-economic situation today. The idea of revelation in biblical religion is tied inextricably to the historical situation of human impoverishment. This point needs to be emphasized because it gives us an idea of the kind of God who is being presented to us by revelation. This God is one who is preferentially disposed toward the poor. The biblical view of society demands that the poor and the needy must be taken care of first. Hence we may conclude that the God of biblical revelation is one whose essence is concern and compassion for those who are in need. This God is one who wants to rescue humans from the condition of poverty and suffering. This is a God who seeks justice and liberation from any situation of oppression or pain. The Exodus story of Yahweh's redemption of an oppressed people, the prophetic protest against neglect of the poor, Jesus' proclaiming the good news to social outcasts—this theme of divine concern for those who lack power and possessions is too dominant for us to ignore when we ask what God is like. We must enshrine the impressions of redemption from suffering and concern for the needy at the heart of our thinking about God and God's dealings with human beings. The book of Revelation in the Bible, aptly titled, discloses to us a God whose intention it is to "wipe away every tear" and to declare that "death shall be no more." (Rev 21:4)

The fact that the poor and suffering are the ones to whom God is most palpably revealed in biblical religion is evidence that God's concern is that oppression, suffering and poverty be abolished as quickly as possible. The needy and all those treated unjustly must be taken care of before the human adventure into the cosmic and historical future can be fully launched. Before we can move in good conscience toward whatever God's promise holds in store for us and for the universe, those whose basic needs are not yet satisfied must be cared for. There is an urgency in the tone of the biblical accounts of God's acting in history that requires our attending *now*, and not later, to those who are in need and whose human dignity remains unrecognized. Today this would include the homeless, the hungry, the imprisoned, the ignorant, the illiterate, any who are economically, environmentally and politically disadvantaged, the elderly, the sick, people in developing nations whose lives may be negatively affected by our own nations' economic policies, and those whose lives are threatened by sexism, racism and abusive ideologies. To grasp the meaning of revelation in our own context does not require that we transport ourselves beyond our present historical situation. We need not look far at all to find instances of poverty and suffering similar to those through which the divine promise has been revealed in the past. The world is as ripe for the announcement of the good news of the Kingdom of God as it has ever been. The conditions for experiencing anew the power of a revelatory promise are just as much with us today as during the biblical period of human history.

And yet the promised arrival of justice and liberation also seems as remote from realization as ever. We may find ourselves being tempted to repeat the murmuring in the desert by the Hebrew people who became so disappointed that fulfillment of the promise offered to them was still so remote. Why do we have to wait? When will the promise be realized? After all these centuries would not God's Kingdom have come into history more obviously than it has, if it is indeed a reality worth trusting?

We are free to follow this pattern of mistrust which the Bible has laid before us as one possibility. When we hear the prophetic exhortation to make justice and compassion a part of our political and social praxis, we may join voice with the cynical protest that universal justice to the poor is an "impractical" approach to social existence that promotes laziness and undermines the free enterprise system. Or we may follow the other path, the path of life and hope in the promise. This path will persist in the face of all adversity with a concern to make justice incarnate in our social existence now, by whatever means possible. It will not be defeated and discouraged by failure but will continue to trust that in some surprising and unanticipated way freedom and justice still constitute the destiny of all. It may trust in the promise for redemption of human history even in the face of the threat of nuclear disaster. It may be confident that even suffering and death cannot defeat the revelatory promise.

The End of Suffering and Death

The content of the revelation of God's Kingdom includes the conviction that suffering and death do not have a legitimate place in the divine plan for human social existence. In the past a certain strain of Christian theology seemed to be much more tolerant of suffering than biblical religion itself permits. And so an attitude of passive tolerance of social situations where millions of poor live in utter squalor has been implicitly supported as acceptable by a theology or theodicy that has "justified" suffering in its understanding of humanity and God. At times an even masochistic exaltation of suffering has been espoused as the most authentic form of spirituality. Today a passive tolerance of the threat of nuclear war by many Christians seems to be condoned by such a warped theology. Part of the reason for this perverse development in Christian thinking is the dominance of a naive theology of redemptive suffering.

But in what sense can suffering be called "redemptive?" On the surface it seems that biblical religion supports the idea that suffering effects or "causes" redemption. The suffering servant of Second Isaiah is pictured in such a way that his sufferings "heal" the people who had mocked him. And of course the sufferings and death of Jesus are presented as "bringing" us our salvation. Add to this the fact that Christians have at times deliberately brought suffering on themselves, thinking that such self-inflicted suffering would make them more loved and accepted by God. The theme of redemptive suffering has been pervasive in theology and spirituality.

We have to ask, though, in what sense suffering itself can be redemptive and healing. Suffering is, after all, a form of evil, something negative rather than positive. If we tend to look upon it as positive, will we not in a subtle way give it a legitimacy or justification that will make us too tolerant of it? And is not this exactly what has happened, at least at times in some episodes of our religious history? Contemporary theologians such as Jürgen Moltmann and Edward Schillebeeckx, however, have emphasized that such an approach to suffering is biblically and theologically untenable. One major aspect of divine revelation, as it is being interpreted today, is simply that God does not want people to suffer. God is one who aims for the reign of justice, freedom, life, joy, and intensity of experience and beauty. Such a divine reality is intolerant of evil, including suffering. The Biblical narratives are clear testimony to this divine compassion.

What then are we to make of so-called "redemptive suffering," including that of the Christ? I think we would be most faithful to theological tradition if we do not take the expression too literally. After all, the idea of "redemptive suffering" has never been completely clear and has always needed interpretation. Different ages have provided such interpretation in radically different ways. Today, though, theology has reached the point where it seems to be saying more clearly than in the past that God redeems us not because of suffering but rather *from* it and *in spite of it*. Suffering is not itself redemptive strictly speaking. Rather it is the *occasion* through which the divine power to save and liberate becomes most clearly manifest. Situations of utter desperation or "impossibility" are the ones most intimately associated in the biblical narrative with the themes of redemption and revelation. But this association need not be construed as a simplistic causal connection in which suffering is seen as "causing" salvation. Desperate situations are the ones in which the divine power, justice and faithfulness (which are actually operative always, including in situations of normality, health and prosperity) often become most dramatically transparent. In situations of suffering and even death the dominant biblical stories hold up to us a promise that the "God of the living"can never be defeated even by the most hopeless extremes into which our experience leads us. But these situations are not themselves redemptive, and it would be unbiblical to assume an attitude of passive tolerance of them. Instead revelation invites us to assume an attitude of hope that there is a way out of such impossible situations.

An example of the biblical hope in redemption from absurd suffering is given in John's Gospel when people ask Jesus whether the infirmities of a certain man are the result of the man's or his parents' sin. The question assumed that suffering is always the necessary result of guilt. Jesus' response is in effect to declare the question irrelevant, to disassociate the man's suffering from any attempt to "explain" it, and instead to see the suffering simply as the occasion for the manifestation of the divine power to heal. This brief episode needs to be made central to our understanding of God's attitude toward suffering. Were we to appropriate this attitude ourselves we would be less tolerant of the injustice and suffering that we see around us in our world today.

Conclusion

Once again therefore, as in the previous two chapters, we have been led back to our central theme that the content of revelation is essentially promise. The God whose very essence is a future filled with the eternal pledge of fidelity is promised anew to us in the social impossibilities that seem so hopeless to us today. We can either face these situations with the attitude that no redemption is possible, or we can situate ourselves in solidarity with the poor and with the forgotten sufferings of the past, keeping their memory alive, and set our faces toward a future in which they and we will experience a redemption from suffering and injustice that goes far beyond our own imaginings. As difficult to accept as the latter may seem in terms of our sense of "realism," it is clearly the one enjoined upon us by the revelatory promise of biblical faith. At the same time, it is likewise hardly possible to call "realistic" any social vision that leaves out the poor, the oppressed and the memory of the sufferings of the past. At least the image of the Kingdom of God can claim a comprehensiveness and breadth that political, social and economic planning ordinarily do not possess. Because it does not repress the memory or awareness of the most desperate it seems to be more aware of the realities of social existence than other social ideals that have been proposed. However, the only way we shall ever find out whether it is indeed a workable image is to place our trust in it and "try it out" for ourselves. As long as we have not ourselves surrendered to its promise and demands we are really not in a position to estimate its power or plausibility.

Our social situation is redeemed only in promise, and our own active praxis of justice in fidelity to this promise is the social "policy" enjoined on us by revelation. A "promissory" fulfillment may not seem to be an adequate solution, especially if we are concerned that our own plans for the good society be actualized in full, here and now. And yet an unflagging trust in the divine promise of social fulfillment is, even from the point of view of "practicality," the only attitude that can adequately respond to our "impossible" dilemma of utopian naivete on the one hand or cynicism on the other. Fidelity to the revelatory promise prevents our concluding that the present social order has already met all the demands of justice, and at the same time our hope in the promise delivers us from the temptation to despair of history's and society's possibilities. Faith views God's promise as itself the adequate solution to both injustice and despair, the two central impediments to authentic social existence.

5

Religion and Revelation

The religious intuitions of our species have always suggested a wider context for our existence than the historical and the social. In fact the religions point to a broader horizon even than cosmology. The most comprehensive situation in which we dwell is neither history nor society nor the cosmos, but *mystery*. It is in mystery that history, society and the cosmos are themselves enshrouded—at least according to the broadly shared views of the world's religious traditions.

In our own time, however, the term "mystery" has, like revelation, become problematic. For some the term mystery carries no religious meaning at all. There are differing views on the degree to which mystery is an explicit ingredient in the experience of people today. Some hold that we live in an age of the "eclipse of mystery." Others are convinced that for the most part people have at least some sense of a dimension of mystery and that therefore religion, understood broadly as a "sense of mystery," still lives on with almost the same degree of explicitness as it has in the past. And still others maintain that mystery has no reality at all, that "mystery" is a notion made up by those who are fleeing from the immediate givenness of the natural, secular or empirical world and that science will eventually eliminate mystery altogether. This third position would hold that there are only "problems," not mysteries, and that in principle all problems are capable of a purely human solution.

The "religious" sense that there is a dimension of incomprehensible and inexhaustible mystery beyond the immediately given world has been predominant throughout most of human history. And though it is being challenged by secularistic culture today, a case may be made that a sense of mystery still lives on in *all* of us at some level of awareness. This general intuition of mystery may be brought to explicitness if we look at certain kinds of questions that differ from the ordinary but which we are quite likely to ask only at the "limits" of our ordinary problem-solving. I am referring to what have sometimes been called "limit questions."[1]

Limit questions arise at the "margins" of our pragmatic concerns and thus open us up to an "other than ordinary" dimension of reality. They are distinct from our usual questions because of their apparently unsolvable nature. For example, a scientist may be totally occupied in trying to solve a specific problem, perhaps spending years attempting to get to some answer. Suddenly this scientist finds himself or herself asking: "Why do I have this passion for the truth? Why should I do science at all?" These are limit questions, and obviously they cannot be solved by science itself. They are "off-limits" to scientific inquiry. In fact they are questions that will never admit of a secure and final solution. They are instead questions that continuously "threaten" ordinary consciousness. They open it up to the domain of what may be called mystery. This dimension of mystery hovers at the boundary of all of our everyday questioning, even though for the most part it remains unnoticed, in humble retreat from our grasping, problem-solving interrogations.

Mystery shows up at the limits of our ethical concerns as well. We may be bothered with the problem of whether this or that action is a violation of the sacredness of life; or we may be worried about whether a particular action is just or unjust; or whether a particular choice is the violation of a promise, etc. These are ethical problems, and we may spend considerable time and energy attempting to resolve them. But quietly, unobtrusively surrounding these ethical preoccupations is the dimension of mystery. We may become explicitly aware of this

---

[1]For the following discussion of limit questions I am indebted especially to David Tracy, *Blessed Rage for Order* (New York: The Seabury Press, 1975), pp. 91-118.

dimension when we notice ourselves asking these limit questions: "Why should we be so concerned about violating life at all?" "Why should we make justice the criterion of our actions?" "Why keep promises at all?" When we ask these questions we have passed beyond the boundary of ethics and have entered into a different arena. The name we may give to the mode of discourse that most appropriately addresses these limit questions is "religion." Religion gives people an "ultimate" answer to the questions why they should be ethical, love justice and remain faithful. It carries them into the realm of mystery toward which all of our limit questions seem to point.

In the area of politics, to give another example, our everyday preoccupations are concerned with whether this or that policy is best for our political life. And we may be almost completely consumed by particular political problems, spending most of our time looking for solutions to them. But it may happen occasionally, especially in times of frustration, that our attention is diverted to an encompassing and "unsolvable" set of questions: "Why should we be so concerned about politics at all? What good does political involvement do in the final analysis? Is there any meaning to political life?" Again, these are the limit questions that seem to seek out another dimension than that of our everyday concerns. They suggest that there is an unconquerable depth of mystery that lurks beneath the surface of all our ordinary engagements and that always seeks to break through more explicitly into our awareness.

In addition to the limit questions through which mystery becomes transparent to our minds there are also limit *experiences* (sometimes called marginal or boundary experiences) that propel us beyond the everyday in an even more impressive way. We come up sharply against the limits of our existence whenever we experience fate, death, guilt or the threat of meaninglessness. The experience of tragic circumstances, of pain and loneliness cannot help but turn our questioning from the trivial to the profound. "Why me?" "Why do I have to die, to suffer, to be lonely?" "Is there any final meaning to my life?" "Why am I here at all?" Such questions arise, however, not only in the face of negative experiences. They also come to the surface in times of great joy and fulfillment. In both tragedy and ecstasy, and often in the midst of very ordinary experiences, these ultimate questions emerge and allow us to come into more explicit contact with mystery. Even in a secularized epoch of history the dimension of mystery is not completely hidden.

In the course of human existence it has been the role of "religion" to provide the "answers" to our limit questions and to illuminate our boundary experiences by placing them in a larger than ordinary context. Religion does this especially by way of symbols and stories, as well as by ritualistic actions that give bodily and dramatic expression to the meanings inherent in symbols and stories. In the symbols, myths and rituals of religion people have been told why they are here, why there is pain and suffering, why life, justice and promise-keeping are valuable, what their destiny is, why truth is worth pursuing. But the religious "answers" have not come with the same degree of certitude and security that answers come to our everyday problems. As I have said, religion uses the language of symbol, and it is precisely in symbols that the dimension of mystery seems to dwell. It is especially through symbols that mystery "reveals " itself to us.

Broadly speaking, a symbol is anything through which we are given a glimpse of something else. By saying one thing directly a symbol or symbolic expression says something else indirectly. The indirect or symbolic meaning, however, is never quite clear. The symbol points us to the meaning, and the meaning needs the symbol in order to communicate itself to us, but it can never be fully translated into non-symbolic propositions. For example, a rock is, directly or literally speaking, a hard, durable and relatively immovable object. Now when I say "so and so is a rock" the term "rock" has taken on a symbolic (metaphorical) meaning. I could say "that person is someone you can rely on" or "she is solid," "he is durable," or "he is immovable." But when I attempt to translate "that person is a rock" into such non-symbolic statements something is lost. I am not saying nearly as much nor as forcefully by breaking the expression down into these literal fragments. There is a fullness of meaning in any original symbolic expression that can never be adequately translated into a series of direct propositions. There is indeed something mysteriously inexhaustible about symbols.

It is easy to see why religions employ symbols as their primary language. Mystery and symbols naturally go together. The horizon of mystery to which religious expression points discloses itself to the religious person or community by way of symbols (and their mythic and ritualistic embodiments). For this reason we can say that *revelation universally has the character of symbolic communication.*[2] In its most general sense "revelation" means the breaking through of the dimension of mystery into our ordinary awareness. And it is especially through the intrinsically revelatory medium of symbols that this unconcealment of mystery occurs. In this sense revelation takes place in some manner in all religions.

The secularistic view of symbols, however, is usually one of skepticism about their revelatory status. Do symbols really reveal anything other than our own subjective or social longings or ideologies? Under the influence of scientism, the Enlightenment's exaltation of reason, modern philosophy and the suspicions cast by social science many intelligent people today suspect that religious symbols are no more than psychic or social "projections." That is, symbols seem to be illusions invented by our childish desires for a comforting world, and they may have nothing to do with "reality." Developments in philosophy, psychology and other social sciences have conspired to make even the religious at times doubtful about the capacity of symbols to put them in touch with the mystery of ultimate reality. And some modern thinkers, following ideas of Nietzsche, Marx and Freud, have taught that religious symbols in particular are deceptive expressions of underlying wishes, prejudices or weakness.

There is much of significance in this modern suspicion of symbolic expression. For we must admit that at times our symbols are overlaid with childish desires and self-serving ideology. Our symbolic language remains in perpetual need of critical examination. To the religious attitude, however, it is primarily through symbols (and their unfolding in myth and ritual) that the ultimate, transcendent mystery of the universe becomes transparent. Laden as these symbols inevitably are

[2]See Avery Dulles, *Models of Revelation* (Garden City, New York: Doubleday & Co., 1983), pp. 131-54.

with ambiguity and suspect human wishing, the religious mind nevertheless believes them to be irreplaceable disclosures of the mystery of ultimate reality. In short, symbols are *revelatory* at the same time at which, when viewed purely psychologically, they appear to be no more than fantastic projections.

From within a purely empirical framework, which puts aside for the moment the believer's faith in the veracity of revelation, symbols seem to be no more than constructs of the human imagination. Like the content of our dreams, the Hindu pictures of Krishna, the native American's belief in Wakan Tanka, and the Christian's image of the risen Lord can all be psychologically "explained" as arising out of wishful thinking. And suppose one goes beyond this psychological observation and maintains—of course this too is a belief—that the empirical-psychological point of view is the *only* valid one. In that case the symbols are not only explained, but their credibility is "explained away" as well. In other words there is nothing revelatory in these symbols. They are simply mirrors that reflect back to us our own desires.

This is the view of scientism. However, it is possible in principle that the psychological interpretation of religious images and symbols as originating in human desiring in no way rules out some correspondence of the symbols with a "mysterious" and ultimate dimension of reality. Symbols can be realistic, that is, revelatory of the mysterious dimension of reality, even while they are, psychologically speaking, partially rooted in our desires. It is not at all impossible that what looks like pure projection from the point of view of psychology may in some way be revelatory of "being" when looked at theologically. Logically speaking the psychological interpretation of symbols says nothing about their revelatory status.

But what is it that religious symbols reveal or allow to appear? The theological response is that the symbols open up to us the *mystery* of reality. But can we form any clear idea of the mystery that they reveal? By definition we cannot. For symbols by their very nature hide from us the very reality that simultaneously comes to expression in them. They remain essentially ambiguous. They conceal what they reveal. They do not allow what is symbolized to be completely transparent to us. They do not permit us to objectify or master that to which they refer. Instead they pull us into the realm of the mystery they represent, but in doing so they still leave us in the darkness of unclarity. It is impossible to comprehend fully a symbol without destroying it. If we are to understand it at all we must allow ourselves to be mastered by the symbol. In surrendering to it we shall find that it remains an endless source of meaning for us as long as we do not break it down analytically into the trivial fragments of objectifying thought. Our thinking must return again and again to the realm of the symbolic in order to receive nourishment, indeed to find anything of importance to think about at all. An appreciation of the "symbolic life" is a necessary condition for the reception of revelation.[3]

Within the broad domain of symbolic consciousness there have been countless representations of the ultimate mystery in which history, society and the cosmos are seemingly embedded. According to Paul Tillich, a simple key to the plurality and diversity of religions and ideologies throughout human history is the fact that almost any thing, event, person or social group can function as a symbol (and therefore revelation) of the ultimate. Since (as the term "phenomenon" suggests) all phenomena are *appearances* that become manifest out of an encompassing horizon of incomprehensible being, there is something revelatory about everything whatsoever. Everything both reveals and conceals the all-embracing mystery of being. And everything has the potential for disclosing this horizon in an exceptionally revelatory way for a particular group or person at any particular time. Thus we can understand the tendency in religions to adorn animals, rocks, rivers, sacred persons, and special events with privileged symbolic status. All of these can be revelatory of mystery, even though psychology, operating from within a scientific framework, may totally overlook this aspect of symbols.[4]

It is possible to discover, beneath the inevitable layers of childish wishing and escapism that may at times form the upper crust of symbolic consciousness, a long and continuous

[3]See Paul Ricoeur, *The Symbolism of Evil*, trans. by E. Buchanan (Boston: Beacon Press, 1967).

[4]See Paul Tillich, *Systematic Theology*, Vol. I (Chicago: University of Chicago Press, 1951), pp. 118-28.

straining after mystery on the part of the human race. The religious quest has for generations without end sought to bring the horizon of mystery into view. The thirst for mystery has been unquenchable, and it has perennially spurred the adventurous search by mystics, seers and ordinary people for the realm of the inexhaustible within which alone they would find the objective of their search. But the mystery has continually eluded the symbolic quest even while it manifests itself fleetingly to the seekers. It is almost as though the mystery were saying to us: "I cannot be grasped fully by your symbols. Your representations of me are too narrow. Seek wider and more transparent symbols." But our quest usually ends far short of this breadth and transparency. We often take our present symbolizations as though they were final and adequate. In biblical religion such a reduction is called idolatry.

Mystery and Special Revelation

In terms of the long human search for adequate representations of the universally intuited dimension of mystery we may now gain more understanding of what Christian theology means by a "special" historical revelation. For Christians too are part of this long human search for mystery. They believe, however, that the ultimate mystery that underlies and transcends the world is made decisively manifest in the person of Jesus the Christ. To Christian faith Jesus is the decisive symbolic revelation of the ultimate mystery of the universe and history. This special symbolic representation of mystery is, of course, part of a larger set of biblical narratives telling in many ways about the presence of God and the divine promise in history. But in Jesus Christian faith perceives what has been called a decisive, final and universal revelation of the mystery of the universe.

In the history of Israel, as we saw earlier, the ultimate mystery of the universe is grasped primarily by way of the narration of historical events that promise future fulfillment. Especially in the story of the momentous *event of liberation* called the Exodus the Hebrew people felt the revelation of the mystery of God. So central was this event, since it made the difference between extinction and survival for them, that their idea of ultimate mystery could never again be divorced from the experience and the story of being set free. The idea of God in biblical religion is essentially that of one who promises and bestows freedom. It is this liberating mystery that shines through, in different ways at different times depending on historical circumstances, in all of the biblical stories of God. Do we still experience the ultimate mystery of our lives fundamentally as *liberation*?

In the Christian context the central symbol through which the divine liberating mystery is revealed to the faithful is the man Jesus who is called the Christ. To understand what God is essentially like, believers are invited to look at this man and his liberating works as they are represented in the Gospel narratives and the other Christian writings and traditions. In John's Gospel Philip asks Jesus to show the disciples the mysterious "Father" who has been announced by Jesus. The fourth Gospel portrays Jesus as responding to this request by pointing to himself: "Have I been with you so long, and yet you do not know me, Philip? He who has seen me has seen the Father." (Jn 14:9) To see Jesus, and to participate in the Jesus story, is to experience the mystery that he calls "Father." Religiously speaking Jesus is the symbolic manifestation of the mystery that surrounds us. His life, words, deeds, death and the impressions on his followers of his living anew after his death all constitute more than just historical data. The total Christ-event is *symbolically* revelatory of the ultimately mysterious horizon of our existence.

In the story of Christ the cloud of mystery intimated in our boundary experiences and limit questions is given a personal face that summons us to a distinctive type of response that can be called the Christian life. Followers of Christ have experienced in their relation to him an unsurpassable encounter with mystery. They are thus given the possibility of naming and relating intimately and personally in a new way to the dimension of mystery that underlies all of human experience. They are given a "way" by which to respond to the limit questions and experiences that often leave us utterly perplexed. They have found nothing in their experience that better translates for them their native sense of life's mysteriousness into a form that dispels the darkness and resolves the ambiguity that always lurks beneath the surface of life.

This does not mean, however, that they are permitted to isolate themselves from the ongoing human quest for mystery or from the many and various symbolic traditions that speak of mystery in other ways. Christian theology today is becoming more and more comfortable with the view that the symbols of all the religions are in some sense revelatory of the same God that biblical religion discloses in its own manner. The fundamental "mystery of the universe" is free to reveal itself in any number of ways, and no tradition can claim an exhaustive unfolding of this mystery whose very essence is understood in biblical tradition as freedom. Even in those cases where the idea of God is absent (as in Theravada Buddhism) each religious expression has the potential for disclosing in a unique and unrepeatable way an aspect of the universal mystery. There is no basis in Christian teaching for a narrow-minded sectarianism which holds that there is only one access to the mystery out of which the world exists. There is no reason why the Christian cannot learn much about God by "passing over" into other traditions and trying to see the world as others see it.[5] Indeed the injunction of neighborly love would seem to demand such empathy. By losing themselves in others' perspectives Christians may find themselves and God anew. Fidelity to the spirit of Jesus' teachings is realized not in possessive clinging to one's own tradition but in placing it in dialogue with others. The age of religious narrowness is over, at least in principle. Christians can say this even though it is obvious that the forces of fundamentalism are growing stronger today, often hand in hand with fierce nationalistic revivalism. In our present historical situation it is most urgent for the sake of preventing the shrivelling of the emerging pluralistic sense of the mystery of reality that religions resist the temptation to such retrenchment. If mystery is to take hold of human consciousness today we must be open to the many ways in which it is symbolized.

This means that Christians are not obliged to hold that the

---

[5]See John Dunne, *The Way of All the Earth* (New York: The Macmillan Company, 1972).

mystery of their lives is in every detail disclosed by way of the experience of Israel and the person or teaching of Jesus, or in the Scriptures, or in tradition. A close reading of these sources of the Christian idea of God will itself show that none of them has imposed such a restriction on Christian faith. Instead the classic sources of theology have always maintained that the inexhaustible mystery of God remains hidden even while it is being revealed. If this is the case, if God is truly a hidden God, then there is no reason why aspects of God that remain hidden from us in our experience of specifically Christian history and symbolism cannot become genuinely transparent to us in our association with other religions and traditions.

It is no secret that in the past such a "tolerant" perspective on revelation seemed hardly permissible to Christians. But just as new understandings of cosmos, history and society have compelled us to revise our views of revelation, so also our new understanding of the world's pluralistic religious situation demands a similar rethinking. We have barely begun this enterprise in Christian theology, though it is one of the most urgent theological exigencies of our time. We may therefore be forgiven if our first efforts are somewhat awkward.

What can the Christian belief in "special revelation" possibly mean when it is articulated in terms of the penumbra of mystery that constitutes the widest context of our existence and which is testified to universally in human religious experience and symbolism? "Special revelation" means first of all and most obviously the specific "face" this mystery takes to the community of those who adhere to specifically *Christian* faith. We have said that wherever mystery becomes manifest there is revelation. This is what is meant by the theological notion of "general revelation." As Paul Tillich has put it, revelation is the "manifestation of the mystery of Being." And all religion is revelatory in this sense. But to the Christian there is a "special," "decisive," or "final" character to the revelation of God in Jesus who is called the Christ. How can we reconcile this emphasis on the definitiveness of Christ with our acknowledgement of and continual openness to the general revelation of mystery given to our universe, to human existence and especially to religious experience?

In the writings of the New Testament and in Christian

tradition we are told, often in so many words, that the fullness of revelation occurs in Jesus the Christ. Can a Christian honestly engage other religions while clinging to this particularity of belief? Avery Dulles quite correctly says: "Without repudiating its own foundations Christianity cannot deny the permanent and universal significance of Jesus Christ as the preeminent 'real symbol' of God's turning to the world in merciful love."[6] But, as Dulles and other theologians also insist, such a confessional statement does not preclude the possibility of open dialogue and genuine willingness to learn new things about mystery from other positions.

Can we openly and honestly encounter the mystery of the universe in other traditions without being willing to surrender the claim of the universal significance of Christ? One way of responding to this contemporary theological quandary is to think out more fully the implications of a belief in "the universal significance of Christ." This expression entails, among other things, that we need never fear being open to the truth, no matter how foreign it appears in terms of our present understanding. In Chapter 7 I shall discuss in another context the relation between our desire for truth and the quest for revelation. But in the present chapter it is important also to say a few words about this relationship in connection with the problem of how to unite faith in the universal significance of Christ with an openness to non-Christian religious traditions.

If Christ is universal in his presence and significance, the Christian fortified with this belief can venture forth into the realm of the foreign and unknown without fear of opening himself or herself to the truth, no matter what this truth may be. Instead of being an obstacle to be overcome, belief in the universal significance of Christ can actually open up areas that would otherwise be overlooked. For if the name "Christ" stands for anything, it means openness, compassion, understanding, acceptance, tolerance, justice and freedom. Abiding in this name allows no construal of revelation as a restrictive body of truths that prohibits us in any way from exploring the vast universe of nature, culture and religion. Revelation is not

<hr />

[6]Dulles, p. 275.

meant to draw an impenetrable circle of safety around our minds and lives. And the experience of a "special revelation" in terms of the figure of "Christ" may provide the liberating images in which our consciousness dwells so that it may *break out* into an exploration of the inexhaustible mystery that manifests itself everywhere and especially in the world's religious traditions.[7] To understand this point a brief summary of Michael Polanyi's theory of human knowing might be helpful.

There are two kinds of knowing, explicit or focal knowing on the one hand, and tacit or subsidiary knowing on the other.[8] Whenever we become explicitly or focally aware of something, for example another person's face, it is because our awareness is tacitly "indwelling" the particular "subsidiary'" features of that face. Our tacit (or non-explicit) knowledge indwells the countless individual features of the other person's visage, such as the nose, eyes, eyebrows, mouth, texture of skin, and all the subtle attitudes assumed by the face depending on the person's mood at any particular time. Our tacit knowledge quietly indwells these facial subsidiaries and, using them as clues, integrates them into a focal impression that allows us to read the *whole* face as smiling, angry, indifferent, etc. It is only because of the incredibly integrative power of our tacit, indwelling, and subsidiary understanding that we are able to focus explicitly on the face as a whole unit with a specific overall meaning.

A tacit knowledge of particulars underlies all our explicit awareness, of anything whatsoever, including religion. The focal meaning that you find on this printed page, for example, is possible only because your tacit knowing is dwelling in the particular letters and words I am using; and your subsidiary knowing of the sounds of individual letters and the meanings of individual words is now (without your focusing on it)

---

[7] The notion of indwelling in order to "break out" into wider fields of exploration has been developed in the works of Michael Polanyi. For the following see especially *The Tacit Dimension* (New York: Doubleday Anchor Books, 1967), pp. 55-92.

[8] Michael Polanyi, *The Tacit Dimension*. I would prefer to use the term "understanding" instead of "knowing" in many cases where Polanyi uses the latter term. But for the sake of this brief discussion, I shall abide by Polanyi's usage.

integrating the particulars into the explicit meaning you find in my sentences and paragraphs. Now if you turn your focal attention to one or more of the particular letters or words on this page you will notice something quite remarkable. While you are focally attending to one of the letters or words you will thereby have lost touch (for the moment at least) with what the letters mean in a particular sentence or paragraph. You will have become temporarily "alienated" from the overall organic meaning to which the letters and words are jointly pointing. To grasp their meaning you must look *from* the letters and words rather than *at* them. This is because meaning can be found not in the particulars but only in your integrating them into a specific *patterning*. And whenever we turn our focal awareness away from the whole pattern and toward the particulars we lose the overall meaning, at least momentarily. As Polanyi says, we have to attend *from* the particulars *to* the joint or focal meaning. If we attend *to* the particulars we lose the general meaning.

All of our knowledge has this *from-to* structure. That is, we attend *from* the particulars *to* their joint meaning. And we cannot ignore this fact when we are speaking of revelatory knowledge. We would encounter any revelatory meaning only by first dwelling in and relying upon many particular linguistic and symbolic particulars. This point is particularly important when we are placing our own religion's sense of life's meaning, allegedly given to us by a special historical revelation, into an encounter with other traditions' sense of life's meaning, given to them by their own symbolic traditions. What makes it possible for revelation to have meaning for us is that our awareness first of all quietly indwells the particular or subsidiary words, symbols, stories, habits etc. of our biblically based culture. And in faith our awareness integrates these clues into a joint meaning that we may call revelatory. What is revelatory is not the particular clues themselves, for many of them (such as the lexicon of terms used) are shared by others in our culture who are not of our faith. Rather the revelatory aspect resides in the specific focal meaning that issues from a special tacit integration of these clues into a specific pattern with a definite meaning.

A truly revelatory symbolism is revelatory precisely because of its capacity for integrating a multiplicity of clues into new and lifegiving patterns. If our image of Christ functions protectively to inhibit such integration of novelty, then it is no longer functioning in a revelatory manner. Rather it would be operating in a very non-revelatory way. We can test the revelatory resourcefulness of the symbolism in which our consciousness dwells by asking whether it opens us up to the otherness of foreign ideas and traditions, and thus leads toward deeper and wider integrations of meaning, or instead keeps us locked in the narrow fortress of obsession with our own dogmatic certitudes. The power of a tradition to influence the lives of people depends in part upon its capacity to help them assimilate new experiences. The Jesus story, then, would be revelatory for us only to the extent that it is capable of providing the basis for such integration of novelty. And if we look too obsessive *at* this story rather than *with* it and *from* it we shall run the risk of losing its real meaning. Revelation is not a set of propositions to look *at*, but a body of symbols in which we are invited to dwell so that we might look out *from* them at the rest of the world in a more comprehending and open-minded way.

We cannot expect others to grasp the revelatory nature of our "special" faith-integrations if they do not first of all "indwell" the cultural and linguistic elements that are patterned into our own revelatory integrations. And it is highly unlikely that such integrations can occur without some measure of acculturation. Think for example of how difficult it is for most of us Westerners to be moved deeply by images of the Buddha, unless we have been educated to the point of spontaneously indwelling the particular historical, psychological, social and other particulars that are subsidiaries of Buddhist piety. Such images can hardly be revelatory to us until we have learned tacitly to indwell many of the cultural particulars that the Buddhist abides in spontaneously.

We cannot automatically expect others to "see" what we Christians have focally seen in our primary symbol, Jesus the Christ, unless they first share with us a sufficiently common set of subsidiary cultural and linguistic ingredients. And such sharing is often very difficult, not just between East and West, but also between secular and religious, Protestant and Catholic,

Mediterranean Catholic and Irish Catholic, etc. Of course there are fortunately many transcultural clues to meaning (such as smiling, laughing, crying, asserting, demanding, questioning, etc.) that point universally to common meanings. But there are countless other culturally specific experiences that are not easily transferable from one context to another. Such facts must be taken into account in all inter-religious dialogue.

For the most part, however, the world's religious traditions still remain considerably out of touch with each other. This mutual isolation may have been a necessity for a period of time sufficient for them to acquire a certain autonomous identity without which an enriching relationship among them would never eventually become possible. But the time for deeper interrelationship appears now to be upon us. What the outcome of a committed encounter with world religions will be it is impossible to tell at this stage. How the Christian belief in the universal significance of Christ will be understood in the future we simply do not know. What we can assume, however, is that our indwelling of the clues that comprise our revelatory tradition can lead us to break out into a much more adventurous encounter with other traditions than we have allowed in the past.

6

The Self and Revelation

It has often been observed that each of us has a powerful and insatiable longing to be regarded as significant in the eyes of another.[1] This passion for significance is the deeply interior desire that governs our lives, fills our days and shapes our dreams. We could probably understand our actions, thoughts and feelings much better if we would honestly ask ourselves: "Whom am I trying to please and why am I doing so?" An answer to this question would go some distance toward giving us a sense of our own identities.

But of course we do not often ask this question, and as a result we sometimes live out our lives in unawareness of the kind of performance we are putting on for unacknowledged others in order that we might prove to be of value in their (imagined) regard. And in the course of our lives the sense of who we really are in the depths of our selfhood may virtually elude us.

It would be a "devastating release of truth," Ernest Becker maintains, to admit our need to be heroic before another or others, and thus to become conscious of what we are doing to earn our self-esteem. It would involve our clarifying for ourselves what powers we are living by and to what degree we are possibly subservient to these powers. Most of us, Becker

[1]For example, Ernest Becker, *The Denial of Death* (New York: The Free Press, 1973)l; and Sebastian Moore, *The Inner Loneliness* (New York: Crossroad Publishing Co., 1982).

insinuates, never get very far in this self-analysis. Very few of us break away from the powers that we are secretly trying to please in order to feel significant. And so we sometimes live narrow, restricted lives because the powers we try to please are usually so narrow and restricted themselves.[2]

Why do we engage in these "heroics?" Becker's answer is an ancient one: we are simply trying to escape the threat of death. In a more general sense we may say that we are trying to cope with our vulnerability which manifests itself not only in our mortality but also in our bodily existence as such. From very early in life we sense the annihilating implications of our bodily existence, and we are understandably terrorized and overwhelmed by this awareness. So we strive to hide our fragile existence in persons, things or institutions that seem to promise us protection from having to face our naked dependency and eventual death. We strive unconsciously to find beings that can give us the significance for which we long and that can compensate for our underlying sense of the precariousness of our existence. From the time of infancy we immortalize our parents in a special way, placing around them an aura of invincibility that can apparently conquer the threat of death and the sense of our own powerlessness. And when we "outgrow" our parents we simply "transfer" the aura of invincibility onto others, such as a spouse, a lover, a nation, a job, a boss, an institution or our career. We attempt desperately at times to please these "powers" that shield us from our weakness and mortality. We perform our "heroics" for them so that we might gain their approval and a sense of our own significance in the face of death and finitude. And in ways of which we are not usually aware, we shape our "characters" in accordance with their demands.

I think we should be quite tolerant and sympathetic toward such heroics. The terror of death and finitude is normal, and it is no wonder that we seek some sort of security in the face of the void's constant threat to our existence. The need to feel significant is built into us, and it would be silly to deny it. That is not the problem. The problem—and this is everybody's life

---

[2]Becker, *passim.*

problem—is deciding *before whom or what* we shall perform our heroics and carry out our longing for significance. Before whom or what?

The social world in which we are each embedded and in which our personalities are shaped provides us with all sorts of opportunities to perform our heroics in order to feel significant before others. Indeed society is in part a "system of heroics"[3] constantly holding out to us criteria of self-worth. Parental, familial, political, academic, athletic, artistic, ecclesiastical and many other dimensions of our social environment give us all the opportunities we need to convince others of our importance. By abiding in these different circles, and performing before others within them, our need for significance may be temporarily satisfied. We achieve the recognition that we understandably desire, and we find it sufficient to live off of this recognition for long periods of time, sometimes indefinitely.

We need not condemn ourselves or others for engaging in this quest for acceptance. The longing to be accepted is part of our human nature. And yet it may and often does happen that the kind of significance provided by our immediate environments with their various systems of heroics and criteria of worth is not enough to stave off our anxiety in a satisfying way. The old question, "Am I truly significant to someone?", rises up again and again from what has been called our "inner loneliness." And the quest for some relief from this loneliness goes on and on. It has gone on since the beginning of our human history, but it began to intensify in modern times. Today it is an all-consuming quest, and it takes very little awareness of contemporary cultures and life-styles to notice that the problem of loneliness is the most pressing problem each individual has to cope with.[4] How does one find significance in the face of our vulnerability to death? And how do we relieve the loneliness we usually have to fall back on when we realize that the "powers" in front of which we put on

---

[3] The expression "system of heroics" is employed by Becker as a central concept in *The Denial Of Death.*

[4] I am indebted especially to Sebastian Moore's book, cited above, for this discussion of loneliness.

our heroic preformances may offer no final protection against our annihilation?

We may find that our striving to win esteem in any particular context has another side to it that I have not yet mentioned. I am referring to the fact that the fervent effort to please the powers we rely on for our sense of self-esteem may cause us to deny those aspects of our existence that seem to conflict with the conditions of worth held out to us by family, school, fraternity, sorority, church, government, place of employment, etc. This denial of some sides of ourselves is not surprising. Most social scientists are aware that each of us has an aspect of our personality that does not easily fit into the social settings in which we find ourselves. There is always an "identity fragment," an "unsocialized component of the self," a core of "subjectivity," a hidden and impenetrable "individuality" that will not or cannot correspond to the criteria of worth implied in our heroic systems. Depth psychologists have testified in varying ways to the presence of what I shall call for the sake of simplicity our "hidden selfhood." We need not detail their observations here. Suffice it to say that they are all aware of how we sometimes "repress" or push out of consciousness that side of our self that cannot live up to the demands of social heroics. Through this repression an inner division is established within us, and much of our energy is consumed in keeping our hidden selfhood separate from our socialized selfhood. So sorely do we long for approval, though, that we are capable of maintaining this internal division for long periods of time, and we may learn to grow somewhat comfortable with the self-deception implied in it. Beneath the surface, however, there lurks a loneliness that may grow more and more burdensome even as we win the esteem of others. How can one find significance in the depths of this loneliness?

The quest for revelation, as interpreted from the perspective of individual selfhood, may be understood as the quest for this significance. It is the longing for a "word" that might convince us that our quest for significance is not in vain. It is the search for a word that does not condemn us for undertaking the apparently self-centered search for acceptance but which reminds us of the false promises offered by some of our normal means of relieving our loneliness. Christians have believed, ever since the time of the first disciples, that such a word is incredibly offered to us in the life, person, and teachings of Jesus who is called the Christ. It is a word given not only to the universe, society and history, which we have already looked at, but also to the hidden, private freedom and selfhood of each one of us. Throughout the Christian centuries interpreters of this word have emphasized that such a revelation can take root in our universe and in society and its history only if it takes root first of all in the life of the individual. It is indeed a word of promise addressed to all, but it has to be received first by individuals who then feel called to share it with others.

Sebastian Moore points out that our individual loneliness

> . . . yearns for a mysterious communion that would relieve it. In search of this mysterious other, I do not look away from, or outside, the world, but beyond it. And this really means that in me the world looks beyond itself. I represent and experience the loneliness of all being. In me the galaxies hunger for God. In me all the world craves his companionship.[5]

The quest for revelation is the quest for this companionship, a quest that has its origins in the cosmos itself and that now in our unique individualities reaches out for a climactic friendship that delivers not only each person but the entire universe from its loneliness. The Christian faith has always maintained that in Christ the promise of divine companionship is offered in a clear and momentous way to the universe by way of each person.

It is quite possible to see why the early followers of Jesus found in his life, words, actions and death a definitive and unsurpassable disclosure of a divine friendship that signifies the real importance of each individual. Jesus' mission was to tear through the obscuring veil of social and religious systems of heroics in order to bring to light the notion of a love that places no criteria of worth on us. His gestures, parables and words all relativized the reigning systems of heroics. He

[5]Moore, p. 104.

wanted people to realize that they cannot earn their sense of significance, no matter how hard they try, since they are already accepted as important. Our quest for "identity" by proving ourselves worthy through strict obedience to contrived religious and ethical legalisms is futile. Our identity as eternally significant, as persons intimately cared for by an unsurpassable mystery of love is already established. And this identity is sufficient for us. No familial, ethnic, religious, political or economic ladder-climbing will make us one iota more intrinsically significant than we already are.

Almost any of Jesus' actions and parables make this point. Recent biblical scholarship instructs us that Jesus' reference to God as "Abba," which is a trust-filled term of address to one's "father," a name of intimacy and deep affection, already contains the nucleus of the Christian revelation. The term "Abba" already signifies that each person is cared for in a way that should evoke a child-like sense of trust, as well as an awareness of the futility of our attempts to secure our existence by way of heroics. Jesus' parables all unfold this central idea.

As just one example we might look briefly at the parable of the "Laborers in the Vineyard."

> . . . the kingdom of heaven is like a householder who went out early in the morning to hire laborers for his vineyard. After agreeing with the laborers for a denarius a day, he sent them into this vineyard. And going out about the third hour he saw others standing idle in the market place; and to them he said, "You go into the vineyard too, and whatever is right I will give you." So they went. Going out again about the sixth hour, he did the same. And about the eleventh hour he went out and found others standing; and he said to them, "Why do you stand here idle all day?" They said to him, "Because no one has hired us." He said to them, "You go into the vineyard too." And when evening came, the owner of the vineyard said to his steward, "Call the laborers and pay them their wages, beginning with the last, up to the first." And when those hired about the eleventh hour came, each of them received a denarius. Now when the first came, they thought they would receive more; but each of them also received a denarius. And on receiving it they grumbled at

the householder, saying, "These last worked only one hour,
and you have made them equal to us who have borne the
burden of the day and the scorching heat." But he replied to
one of them, "Friend, I am doing you no wrong; did you not
agree with me for denarius? Take what belongs to you, and
go; I choose to give to this last as I give to you. Am I not
allowed to do what I choose with what belongs to me? Or do
you begrudge my generosity?" (Mt 20:1-15)

One clear implication of this story is that the criteria of worth
enjoined by the economic assumptions of the laborers are
relativized by the generosity of the owner of the vineyard.
Jesus' startling (and obviously unsettling) teaching is that the
Kingdom of God consists of relationships like those disclosed
in the parable. Our individual efforts cannot win God's love for
us. God's love does not depend upon our fulfilling certain
conditions of worth in order to prove ourselves worthy of it.
The incredible fact is that an unconditional love has already
been offered to us. All we have to do is accept it. Of course
accepting it fully may be more difficult for us than trying to
earn it. For such a trust requires an admission on our part that
we cannot earn our justification by our own efforts. Perhaps
we can now see once again why the revelation of God enters
our history especially through the sensitivities of the poor, the
sinners, the desperate who are in the "impossible" situation of
no longer being able to prove themselves worthy of anything.
Such individuals can only open themselves to the promise of
acceptance in spite of their powerlessness.

The otherness, the contradiction and the undreamed of
implications of revelation are nowhere more obvious than in
the shocking disclosure by Jesus of a love whose bestowal does
not depend upon moral, spiritual or any other type of
achievement on our part. This idea clashes so sharply with the
"normal" world of social heroics that it is hardly possible for it
to have bubbled up "naturally" or accidentally from the latter
alone. Its inconceivable and "impossible" nature has led
believers to see it therefore as a revelatory "interruption" of the
fabric of normality. It would be very difficult to account for
this idea simply in terms of sociological or rational analysis
alone. In fact it clearly goes against the grain of how we know

society to work, and it is hardly an idea that a philosopher interested in "reality" could arrive at by cogitation alone. If we ponder it, the belief that our value does not depend on our achievements can completely upset our usual way of looking at the world and at ourselves. And it can have troubling, even revolutionary implications for society's self-understanding. Its truly startling nature makes it an acceptable candidate for claiming the status of "revelation."

Jesus must have known this. Perhaps that is why he insisted that one must become like a little child to accept the idea. A child simply opens himself or herself to receive gifts and does not look around immediately to ask if the gifts have been deserved. Typically the child simply accepts a gift with joy and gratitude and shows little concern with the question of meriting it. Such, according to Jesus' teaching, should be our own response to the good news of our abiding and intrinsic significance.

Sebastian Moore rightly suggests that we need not repress in ourselves the apparently selfish and even narcissistic passion to be recognized, cherished and deeply desired by another. This child-like layer of our desiring is a permanent and essential part of our make-up, and to root it out would be an act of violence toward ourselves. The "puritanical" or stoical exhortation to withdraw our desire for significance in the eyes of another and learn in the spirit of tragic "realism" to accept the indifference of the universe has long been a strongly appealing "philosophy of life." It seems to have a touch of "sobriety" and a taste for courage that satisfies the affinity for tragedy that we may all harbor in our souls. As I pointed out earlier, the tragic vision of existence has an allure that remains a constant temptation for us. And many endearing figures in our human past and present have been able to "adjust" to the world by "giving up" or "working through" their childhood longing for significance in the eyes of another. In our own times psychoanalysis and many derivative psychologies have encouraged people toward this stoic resignation.

I cannot deny that this exhortation to undergo a thorough "ascesis of desire" has brought a sort of contentment to many. And yet I cannot help but wonder also if such resignation, courageous as it seems to be, is not sometimes accompanied by a premature despair about the promise of what our full possibilities are. Is this despair perhaps a shield against a deeper possibility of becoming human before another? At least it seems to be so when placed in an encounter with the promissory word that there is an ultimate companionship capable of dissolving our loneliness and of reminding us of an inherent significance that we had not been remotely capable of imagining on our own. This word presses us to hope for the unimaginable and to trust in things that by simple human calculation are impossible. And if anything appears impossible to us from our vantage point within any system of heroics, it is that our significance does not come from the system itself, but from a source beyond it. A "word" that convinces us of this transcending value would awaken (or reawaken) in us the primordial urge to feel fully significant. Instead of urging us to control such a desire, as tragic thinking does, it would release it. Such a liberating word could understandably be called "revelatory."

In presenting these elemental Christian teachings in class I have often found that students are quick to ask the following question: if one took seriously Jesus' message that we do not have to earn our sense of feeling good about ourselves, would this not allow for an unrestrained, licentious life, believing that we are loved regardless of our behavior? I think the answer to this question is relatively simple. Jesus has no fear at all that those who sincerely accept his "wild" vision of a companion-God who regards us as unimaginably significant will be inclined toward "immoral" conduct. If indeed we could in trust accept his idea of God and of our identity as "friend" in the mind of this God, our response would be one of such gratitude that it would actually lead us toward enhancing others' sense of their own intrinsic significance and of their own being similarly befriended. It would arouse in us a new sense of liberty, and it would lead us toward a life of sharing our freedom with others (as St. Paul's life illustrates). In other words it would lead us toward, rather than away from, a truly ethical life. It would be a difficult life. It would bring us into constant conflict, as it did Jesus, with those systems of heroics that enslave and intimidate people at the same time they bestow on them an illusory and fragmentary significance. And it would bring us into confrontation with the injustice that has its roots in the deceptions of social heroics. It would hardly be the occasion for unethical existence. But it would allow us to put the ethical side of life into a new and liberating perspective. In any case, our ethical aspirations require as a condition for their vitality a basic trust in our own self-worth. So instead of opening the way to moral laxity, a feeling of one's significance would more likely lead us to the living of a better and more caring life for others. Faith in revelation can thus free us from self-preoccupation by giving us the sense that we are already cared for. Only such a conviction can fully allow a life-for-others. Jesus' own life of loving concern for others was made possible by such absolute trust in his being completely cared for by God.

The revelation of an ultimate friendship, however, is not without its own kind of injunction or demand. But the demand is simply that we surrender any attempt to solve the big problems of life all by ourselves. And of course perhaps the biggest problem for us as individuals is that of finding a way to alleviate our "inner loneliness" and to feel significant. Learning to feel that our joys and burdens are being shared by a transcendent "other" may be a difficult process itself, one that for some reason or other we tend to resist, perhaps because it seems "unrealistic." There is no allowance for "cheap grace" in this teaching. It will inevitably prove to be a more demanding challenge than any tragic vision proposes for us.

Conclusion

Looked at from within our fifth circle, that of the privacy of our own personality, "revelation" is the disclosure to us that our native longing for significance has an undreamed of fulfillment in a divine friendship which has already given an eternal validity to our lives. The revelatory word addressed to the hidden subjectivity of each of us is that our longing for significance is not destined to be forever frustrated. Revelation is the disclosure of a being-cared-for that our own efforts are simply unable to bring forth. The reason it may be called "revelation," rather than the simple unfolding of human longings, is that it addresses us with a "word" that we could hardly have dreamed up starting from within the context of our superficial social and personal existence.

It is finally through the *individual's* trust in the truth of being-cared-for eternally that revelation enters into our history and society. Without such an individual response to promise we could not speak of "revelation in history." As I attempted to show in Chapter 2, revelation has a cosmic context that we cannot ignore. Here I would emphasize that God's revelation to the cosmos, a revelation mediated by history, finds its way into the heart of the universe and society especially through the free trust placed by individuals in the promise that there is a fulfillment to their own longing for an inviolable significance.

7

Reason and Revelation

Throughout the preceding chapters I have repeatedly emphasized the promissory nature of revelation. Revelation is fundamentally God's self-revelation. But the infinite mystery we call God can be received by us only as promise. Promise is both the content and the context of revelation. The limited, finite character of ours and the world's existence cannot receive the infinite in a single receptive moment. Thus God's reality (and, therefore, revelation also) cannot be adequately contained by the present or the past, but is located primarily in the realm of futurity. Revelation, in the words of Wolfhart Pannenberg, is the "arrival of the future." And the "arrival" of God, whose essence is "futurity," is experienced presently in the mode of promise. The God of the Bible always addresses us out of the inexhaustible "newness" of the future. And this means that our present religious consciousness must assume the distinctive attitude of radical openness to the future if it is to be properly receptive of revelation. This attitude is called hope.

But is hope in God's promise of an ultimately fulfilling future a *realistic* attitude for us to take? We must finally ask more explicitly than we have up to this point what every reader of this book has probably also asked at times along the way: is not the so-called revelation of a self-giving, liberating and unconditionally loving divine mystery likely to be just another example of wishful thinking? How can it all be true? Does not revelation seem a bit implausible? Without throwing reason to the wind can we honestly think that God speaks to us in history out of an open-ended future of promise? Can an intelligent or "enlightened" person honestly accept the notion that our life is not the one-sided affair of which we spoke in the opening pages?

The idea of revelation in history is intrinsically bound up with Western theistic religious traditions. It is not surprising, then, that as theism has been seriously challenged in the last three centuries so also the idea of revelation has been attacked as equally unrealistic. Ever since the scientific revolution and the age of reason began to dominate the intellectual life of the West there have been important thinkers who have challenged as unscientific and irrational both the idea of God and the notion of revelation. And especially since the eighteenth century even some theologians have doubted that we need the notion of revelation, especially since the natural world seems sufficient evidence of the existence and nature of God. For several centuries the notion of revelation in history has been the subject of a controversy that is still far from resolution.

A significant component of the context out of which the problem of revelation has arisen is what may be called "critical consciousness." This is a modern kind of mentality which tends to be distrustful of any understanding based on "authority" alone or that takes place without the endorsement of reason and especially of scientifically enlightened reason. We live in an age of criticism and its attendant questioning of any symbolic religious awareness. Criticism thrives in the universities of the world today, and it has deeply affected popular culture as well. Its demands and criteria, though often diluted, are spread abroad everywhere. Indeed we might say that criticism is the "spirit" of the intellectual component of our culture.

So imperious have been the demands of critical consciousness in the intellectual communities of the West that today many theologians spend most of their professional time and energy attempting to deal with it. And it is especially the idea of revelation that seems to be at stake. In order to accommodate the spirit of criticsm and its skepticism about "revealed" knowledge some theologians themselves seem to have surrendered the notion of revelation as hopelessly irretrievable today. Or in their efforts to please the princes of criticism they may seem to have divested revelation of those very qualities of authoritativeness, "otherness" and "impossibility" that believers consider indispensable to any revealed knowledge. We must face the fact that in theology today there is much controversy and confusion about the value and verity of the notion of revelation. And much of the confusion occurs as a result of our not knowing quite how to deal with critical consciousness.

Facing "Reality"

What is the goal of this critical consciousness? What is it searching after? And why does it have such a strong appeal? In general we can say quite directly that critical consciousness is characterized by a noble passion for objectivity and truth. Its suspicion of authority, of piety, of faith of all sorts, stems from its interest in being objective and from its cognizance of the capricious tendencies of human subjectivity. It is aware of how easily the human mind is led astray by our biases and wishes, and so it seeks to find the truth independently of every human desire except the desire to know reality. For that reason it esteems "detached" and "disinterested" methods of knowing which seemingly exclude the involvement of persons in the knowing process. Its conviction is that by such an "objective" method our minds will be put more closely in touch with "reality" than would be possible by any sort of "faith" or personal knowledge.

But what exactly is meant here by *reality*? If our concern is to be realistic, then we must have some assumptions both about what constitutes reality and how we go about putting ourselves in touch with it. What we are calling "critical consciousness" must itself be governed by such assumptions. What are they? Any attempt to test whether hoping in a divine revelatory promise is a realistic posture of consciousness must begin by examining such assumptions.

"Critical consciousness" seems to entail a conviction that our ideas are in touch with the real world only if they pass the test of being "verifiable" or "falsifiable" according to methods of observation that are publicly accessible. Its understandable distrust of the ideas and fantasies we are capable of constructing either out of the privacy of selfhood or out of group bias has led it to impugn all ideas that resist some sort of public or communal verification. The methods of logical deduction and induction, and especially scientific method, seem to possess a neutrality and public accessibility that makes them apt measuring rods for the veracity of our ideas. These apparently impersonal methods seem to allow for a minimum of subjective involvement, of taking things for granted, and of flights of fancy. By eliminating as far as possible the element of personal involvement, it seems that our consciousness will more readily open itself without distortive filters to the real world outside our minds. It is little wonder that critical consciousness has enshrined scientific method, with its ideals of detachment and disinterestedness, as its central model for reality-testing.

Such a way of testing the validity of many propositions is unquestionably appropriate. However, there is a logic and a view of reality (what philosophers call a "metaphysics") operative in the realm of revelatory promise and hope that is deeply resistant to the demands of critical consciousness as it is usually understood. Criticism, after all, operates in the realm of the predictable and the probable, of what is plausible according to science and ordinary human experience. It can accept as valid only that for which there are already analogies and precedents that "objective" science can decipher. It works by taking large numbers of identical occurrences and making generalizations from them. A completely novel, unpredictable or unique occurrence would not constitute the basis for such a generalization, and so it would not fall within the purview of critical methods of inquiry. Science is incapable of dealing with the radically new, the unpredictable and the improbable. For that reason the notion of revelation, a notion that we cannot separate from what is considered quite improbable in terms of our ordinary and critical standards of plausibility, seems to contradict critical consciousness. To those for whom criticism is the only measuring rod for "truth," therefore, revelation will inevitably be problematic.

Moreover, critical consciousness is oriented essentially toward what is verifiable in the present or in the past. Scientific method can verify only those hypotheses for which there is a sufficient amount of data available from the records left by the past (such as fossils in evolutionary theory) or observable in the present. On the other hand the "data" upon which the "hypothesis" of revelation is based are for the most part empirically unavailable. For the realm from which Christian faith senses the appearance of revelation is the future. Revelation as the "arrival of the future" is given only in the form of promise. This promise contains a foretaste of the future; but the future is not yet fully present, and so it remains mostly beyond the limits of what is critically verifiable or publicly accessible.

Does this mean therefore that acceptance of or trust in revelation is unrealistic? Are we escaping from reality if we decide to hope in a promise that seems improbable from the point of view of critical consciousness? Certainly it would be inappropriate (if not impossible) to trust sincerely in something we suspect may not be true or realistic. We must at least agree with criticism's wholesome demand that we be true to the real and try to avoid illusons. And we must also adhere to criticism's demand that we test our private aspirations in the context of a community and its sense of reality.

We may realize these demands by way of following a vision and "praxis" of shared hope. Christian faith holds that our abiding within a community founded on hope in God's promise, and actively shaping history through the practice of justice and liberation, is the most "realistic" posture we can take in the world. Such an approach is realistic because the realm of the "really real" or of "ultimate reality" is essentially the future. The past is gone, and the present is only vanishingly "present" before it disappears into the past. The temporal dimension that is the most persistent and "faithful" in bringing freshness and new life into the present is the future. To faith the future is the domain of the "really real." Therefore, facing reality means facing toward the future. And it is especially through shared images of hope that we can turn our faces toward the future. Moreover, the *sharing* of hope with others provides a communal context in which we can continually "test" the plausibility of our aspirations, lest they become purely private fantasies.

At this point we may observe that the question of the truth of revelation converges with the larger question of the reality of God. This is because revelation, in its promissory nature, locates the realm of the divine primarily in the arena of the future. Many contemporary theologians and biblical scholars have repeatedly indicated that the God of the Bible is one whose very essence is futurity. Therefore, approaching the question of the reality of God requires that we ask also about how we would open ourselves most completely to the arena of the future. How can we face the future if it is not verifiable as are the objects of science and ordinary experience?

It seems that only *hope* can orient us toward the fullness of reality if indeed the fullness of reality lies in the future. For hope is an openness to the breaking in of what is completely unpredictable and unanticipated from the point of view of what is considered to be possible by ordinary standards of expectation. Hoping is not the same as wishing. Wishing is a mode of desire that is oriented entirely from the individual's present. It tends to imagine that the future will turn out the way I would like, on the basis of what pleases me now. Wishing, arising from what Freud called the "pleasure principle" can give rise only to fantasies and illusions. But hoping, as a communally shared aspiration, renounces such illusions and opens itself to a future that may turn out to be quite different from the one I wish for. Hoping is openness to the radically new and "impossible" in a way that wishing is not. Hoping, therefore, can be considered a realistic, indeed the most realistic, stance our consciousness can take. Hoping is faith's way of embracing what Freud called the "reality principle." And if revelation means the arrival of the future into the opening that our hope makes in the fragile fabric of the present, then our acceptance of this revelation is consistent with the critical demand that we face reality.[1]

Revelation, though, does not mean the acceptance of notions that are contrary to reason or to science. Much of the modern protest against the notion of revelation stems from a fear that revelation intends to provide *information* that potentially conflicts with reason or science. And since reason

[1]On the distinction between wishing and hoping see H. A. Williams, *True Resurrection* (New York: Harper Colophon Books, 1972), pp. 178f.

and science carry so much authority today, any alternative source of information would be suspect.

But revelation is not informative in the sense of adding horizontally to the list of "facts" in the content of our consciousness. Revelation is the unfolding of a relationship between God and the world. It is not an attempt to usurp the place of our ordinary ways of discovering, and so it does not compete nor conflict with reason or science. Only items in the same category can contradict one another. For example, Newton's ideas may conflict with aspects of Einstein's or Ptolemy's theories of the universe only because they all belong to the same category of thinking, i.e., cosmology. But Newton's science cannot conflict with, say, Shakespeare or Tennyson (unless we mistake the poets for cosmologists), since poetry lies in a completely different mode of thinking from cosmological science.

Likewise, reason and science cannot come into conflict with revelation unless we mistakenly reduce revelation to the category of scientifically informational discourse. Such a reduction is in fact attempted by what is known today as "creationism," or especially "scientific creationism," which presents the biblical accounts of cosmic origins and God's activity as though they were alternative scientific and objectively historical accounts rivaling those of secular science and history. Such a reduction of the biblical material, however, not only unjustly belittles the legitimate achievements of science. It also suppresses the depth of the very notion of revelation by situating it in the category of informational knowledge to which it does not properly belong and which is unworthy of it. Revelation does not give us information that may be placed side by side with scientific knowledge. Instead revelation mediates to us the mystery of God's boundlessly loving relationship to the universe, society, history and personality. Hence it may not be appropriately received in the objectifying mode of scientific method or external historical method. Science and history can provide helpful assistance in understanding the circumstances within which the mystery of God is disclosed. But it would be a misunderstanding of revelation to place its content in the same realm of ideas as those discussed by cosmologists, scientists or historians. Revelation, as the uncovering of God's relation to the world, offers us a content that is much more pervasive and foundational than what we can receive through ordinary ways of gathering information. It will appear as unrealistic only if we try to transform this content into the relatively trivial mode of competing information about the world or history.

Throughout the preceding pages we have emphasized the "foundational" rather than any "informative" character of revelation. In Chapter 2 we noted that revelation is the very well spring and fulfillment of the evolutionary cosmos which science looks at in its particulars. In Chapter 3 we viewed revelation as the gift of a founding promise that brings history into being and that holds out to it the hope of fulfillment. It would here be appropriate to say that revelation also opens up for us a space within which science, reason, historical inquiry and criticism can freely manifest their concern for reality. Revelation is too important to be consigned to the same category as the disciplines which fill in the empty spaces of human ignorance. Instead revelation is what fully opens up for faith the horizon within which human consciousness is set free to pursue the truth through its various disciplinary approaches. Indeed, revelation is the foundation and implicit goal of critical consciousness itself. Let me elaborate on this rather bold proposition.

Revelation and the Desire to Know

We need not conclude our brief discussion of reason and revelation simply by stating that there is no contradiction between them. Such a statement does not go far enough. Rather, we may present a much more positive suggestion as to how they are related to one another: revelation actually *promotes* the deepest objective of critical consciousness, namely, the relating of ourselves and our minds to reality. Establishing this point, however, requires that we get to the heart of what motivates reason, science and critical consciousness. I think Bernard Lonergan has put it best when he calls it "the desire to know." The desire to know is the striving of our consciousness for what is true as distinct from what is merely pleasing. It is our searching to be in touch with reality rather than illusions. It is this desire to know that constitutes the foundation of genuinely critical consiousness.

We can all easily identify a desire to know in the depths of our own consciousness. All we have to do is recognize the fact that we ask questions such as "is this or that really the case?" "Is this or that hypothesis correct?" For example, "is religion true?" "Is revelation valid?" "Is hoping a realistic stance to take?" Such questions are all the evidence we need that we too are motivated by a desire to know. The imperative we all experience to be reasonable and critical is what motivates critical consciousness, and our experiencing this imperative is immediate evidence of our own desire to know reality.

My point here is that not only does revelation not conflict with the demands of reasonableness rooted in our desire to know; it actively promotes our desire to know and its concern for reality. Acceptance of or trust in the revelation of God's unconditional love of the world and of each person actually liberates our desire to know from those elements in consciousness that tend to frustrate it. How is this so?

In the preceding chapter, while speaking of the relationship of Christian revelation to the life of the individual, I emphasized how revelation in principle delivers us from the need for self-deception. By offering us the sense of being given an eternal and inviolable significance, revelation frees us from any need for self-deception. And self-deception is the major obstacle we have to conquer if our desire to know is to reach its objective: reality. For if we cannot be truthful about ourselves we can hardly be truthful in our understanding of others and of the real world around us. It is a psychological truism that self-deception places a distortive filter not only between our native reasonableness and our own selves, but also between our minds and reality as such.

If the desire to know is to be set free to reach the truth, then the first step in such a liberation is the conquering of self-deception. It follows that any transformation in our self-understanding that would erode our tendencies to deceive ourselves would also work in the interests of our desire to know, the one longing within us that is completely intolerant of deceptions and illusions. But as I argued in the last chapter, self-deception arises when our ineradicable desire for significance plays itself out in social situations where we are expected to "perform" in order to gain our sense of self-worth. And it is these situations that inevitably lead to self-deception. Thus the "solution" to the problem of self-deception requires a restructuring of our relations to those social situations and their implied heroics and criteria of worth that may have pressured us into concealing aspects of ourselves in order to gain the approval we seem to need at a very deep level of our being.

A trust in the revelation of our relationship to an ultimate environment of unconditional love is capable of breaking through such situations and exposing the contexts in which self-deception flourishes. If we sincerely trust that the promise of divine fidelity provides the ultimate context within which to live out our lives, we will not feel obliged to cling too tenaciously to immediate social arrangements in order to find the approval we desire. Hoping in an ultimate horizon of fulfillment beyond any we can adequately imagine on the basis of our interaction with society is capable of liberating us from the idolatrous tendency to demand an impossible acceptance from those around us. Instead we can see others' love and fidelity as symbols or sacraments of an ultimate fidelity to promise. And when the others fail us, their weaknesses need not be taken as a major threat to our own sense of significance. Surrendering in faith to the promise of an ultimate and eternal fidelity may then deliver us from the need to "perform" for finite others or to deny those sides of ourselves that do not seem to meet the approval of these others. Such a faith, if it could indeed become actual, would be in the service of the desire to know. In other words, such faith in revelation would be realistic or truthful in a fundamental sense.

Conclusion

What is at issue in this chapter is whether the claims of revelation are in conflict with the desire to know the truth which allegedly animates critical consciousness. Bernard-Lonergan has noted that the fundamental criterion of truth is "fidelity to the desire to know." I have suggested that a trust in the promise of unconditional divine love given by revelation provides the context in which the desire to know can be liberated from the restraints of self-deception. Allowing our consciousness to be taken up, in faith and hope, into a horizon of divine fidelity, allows the desire to know to flow more freely toward its natural objective, truth. Such a surrender in faith and hope seems to me to be faithful to the desire to know, that is to say, truthful. Hence the deepest level of our rationality, the desire to know, is not in conflict with, but is supported by, revelation.[2]

[2] I have worked these ideas out in considerably more detail in my *Religion and Self-Acceptance* (Lanham, Md., New York, London: University Press of America, 1980).

8

Encountering Revelation

We have approached the question of revelation by considering what it might mean in terms of six distinct aspects of our situation. But an important question still remains: how do we come in touch with this revelation? By what channels is it communicated to us? How do we know when the mystery of existence and the promise of God's future has been disclosed to us in our particular lives?

This is not an easy question to answer in just a few pages, so we must be content with a few suggestions that would ideally be developed in much more detail. The first point I would make is that we do not have to move from where we already are in order to encounter the mystery of our lives. This promising, gracious, liberating and accepting mystery already enfolds our existence, perhaps hidden beneath the realities, persons and events we encounter in our everyday experience. And it also lives in the depths of our own selves. We do not have to be transposed to some sacred place or sit at the feet of seers and mystics, though this need not be neglected either. The substance of what we have been calling revelation is already intimately related to us. The question is how aware are we of this intimacy. And how do we reach a deeper awareness of that which has already communicated itself to us?

It is the nature of our human existence that we come to understand ourselves only in community with others. Existence in community is not just accidental to our being as humans. It is constitutive of our existence to be in relation with others.

Moreover, it is natural to any community that it base its very existence and identity on the great myths or stories that narrate how it came into being and what makes it specially significant. Such stories give the members of the community a sense of their origins and destiny, a sense of what is important, a sense of common purpose. It is impossible to live meaningfully except in relation to such communally shared stories.

The particular face that mystery will take for us is inevitably shaped by the narrative traditions that mold the character of the community in which we reside. It is these narrative traditions that provide the material for the symbolic and mythic expressions through which we as individuals come face to face with mystery. Our reception of revelation would seem to require therefore that we indwell a communal context without which the reception of *any* symbolic communication is impossible. Thus there will inevitably be a communal dimension to revelation.

Christians participate in a community of believers, the *Church,* which feeds on the biblical narrative(s) and especially the story of Jesus the Christ. This narrative dimension of revelation is embodied especially in the sacred *Scriptures.* So meaningful are the stories of God's fidelity recounted in the Scriptures that members of the community spontaneously seek to retell them to their children and to others so that they also might indwell the healing images imprinted in the biblical material. The deposit of this continual retelling throughout the centuries is known as *Tradition,* and together with Scripture it provides a normative basis for the community's relating to the revelatory promise out of which it has its being. In this community, with its scriptures, traditions and rituals, Christians find a further extension of the liberating mystery that came to light especially in Christ, and they are aware that a close relation to the community facilitates encounter with the incarnate God who is mediated through the lives of others. They can respect the fact that there are many other pathways to mystery without denying that they belong to a special story of their own.[1] They cannot cease telling of the wonders that

---

[1]See H. Richard Niebuhr, *The Meaning of Revelation,* pp. 32-66.

have happened to them at least, nor can they cease from sharing with others their own sense of the graciousness of mystery as they have experienced it in Christ. The existence of a Church and a teaching tradition to give body to this sharing is both legitimated and necessitated by the intrinsically social, narrative and historical character of revelation.

To those outside of the Christian tradition the story of Jesus of Nazareth may have little if any significance (just as to most Christians today, though this is certainly not praiseworthy, the story of Muhammed's life holds relatively little religious interest). Each religious community has an "internal" memory of its founding events, and this internal memory is characterized by a high degree of religious involvement in the ongoing narration of those events. One does not find such passionate interest in a scientifically detached summary of religious history undertaken in an external manner. Because the internal account lacks the disinterestedness and detachment of a scientific history one might suspect that it lacks "objectivity." However, the internal memory of events cannot be discarded simply because it is always accompanied by enthusiasm and deep feeling. As we saw in Chapter 3, H. Richard Niebuhr has emphasized that the Christian's primary knowledge of revelation is given not through objective reporting but through participation in a community's internal memory of saving events that to outsiders may have little narrative significance. Yet the high degree of religious sentiment that empowers inner history can put us in touch with the reality of revelatory events much more intimately than could a merely objective recounting. Niebuhr gave us the analogy of a man who has recovered his sight by way of a medical operation. As you listen to the healed man's gratefully enthusiastic account of the event of his recovery of sight, you will notice how strikingly it differs from the medical report given by the doctors who performed the operation. Can we say that the medical report with its cool clinical language is more accurate than the healed man's account? Which account puts us more deeply in touch with the healing event? Could we really understand what it means to recover one's sight if we took only the medical report as our source of information?

Of course objective history provides an essential corrective to our tendencies toward personal and group bias. And critical methods of investigation should be embraced by believers. But a purely detached method of knowing (even if it were possible to be purely detached) would not put us in touch with revelation. If revelation is God's self-disclosure, then it would require a deeply personal, participatory reception on our part. In other words, it is questionable whether we could talk seriously of the encounter with revelation without our first having opened ourselves to it in the genuinely prayerful posture of shared trust and hope.

By participation in a community with the internal story of its own "recovery of sight" (recorded especially in the Scriptures and retold in Tradition) Christians are brought into encounter with the promissory words and events that have given them their life and identity to this day. Encounter with the revelation of which Christians speak is mediated by the community of believers who have handed on the revelation in word and sacrament. This community, the Church, is itself founded by the revelatory promise and is itself a sign or "sacrament" of God's fidelity to the promise of an ultimately fulfilling future for the world and history. Participation in the life of such a community provides a special (though not exclusive) "access" to revelation.

And yet, while many Christians are content with a close relation to the Church, many others, especially today, see little connection between their hope in the future and the Church as they know it. The Church often seems out of touch with the deepest aspirations of humanity in our time. And it too often fails to witness in its own internal structure and practice to the justice and liberation that belong to the Kingdom of God whose coming it is its primary mission to proclaim. As mediating revelation it often seems to be a pitiful failure, and sometimes even an impediment to the burning sense of hope and promise that are the essence of the revelation it professes to convey.

It would be naive of us to deny the weaknesses and failings of the community founded on the revelatory promise. For that reason we may decide that criticism of abuses within the Church is essential for the very sake of manifesting our trust in the promise of revelation. Criticism of the Church by its members is not always a sign of lack of faith on the part of discontented Christians. Rather it may well be the expression of a deep desire to transform the Church into a community faithful to God's promise. This transformation would seek to make the Church, in its own life and structures, a model of justice and liberation for our time. If the actual life of a community whose whole reason for being is to witness to the coming of God's Kingdom is itself deeply flawed with unjust practices (lack of due process, sexism, authoritarianism), then it can hardly witness effectively to history's own hope.

Finally, however, it cannot be forgotten that the Church is founded on hope. It would be inappropriate for its members to give up on the Church, to despair and lose heart. In some sense even a deeply flawed Church has kept the memory of God's promise alive and made it possible for us to recover it anew in each age. Within the community called Church we can still come into intimate encounter with revelation. For this we can be grateful as well as forgiving.

BIBLIOGRAPHY

Baillie, John. *The Idea of Revelation in Recent Thought.* New York: Columbia University Press, 1956.

Dulles, Avery. *Models of Revelation.* Garden City, New York: Doubleday & Co., 1983.

Fries, Heinrich. *Revelation.* New York: Herder and Herder, 1969.

Haughey, John C., ed. *The Faith That Does Justice.* New York: Paulist Press, 1977.

Moltmann, Jürgen. *Theology of Hope.*, trans. by James W. Leitch. New York: Harper & Row, 1967.

Moore, Sebastian. *The Inner Loneliness.* New York: Crossroad Publishing Co., 1982.

Rahner, Karl, S.J. *Foundations of Christian Faith.*, trans. by W. Dych. New York: Crossroad, 1984.

Ricoeur, Paul. *The Symbolism of Evil.*, trans. by E. Buchanan. Boston: Beacon Press, 1967.

Thiemann, Ronald F. *Revelation and Theology.* South Bend, Indiana: University of Notre Dame Press, 1985.

Tracy, David. *Blessed Rage for Order.* New York: The Seabury Press, 1975.

Williams, H.A. *True Resurrection.* New York: Harper Colophon Books, 1972.

Index